CHESAPEAKE

REFLECTIONS

About the Artist and Illustrations

Pen-and-ink illustrations on scratchboard copyright © by Dean B. Bennett, Mount Vernon, Maine.

Artist and author Dean B. Bennett has written and illustrated books about the nature of Maine and other New England states for more than thirty years. He illustrates with pen-and-ink, pencil, watercolor and black-and-white and color photographs. His published books include *Maine's Natural Heritage*, *Allagash: Maine's Wild and Scenic River*, *The Forgotten Nature of New England*, *The Wilderness from Chamberlain Farm* (an Allagash history), three children's books and *Nature and Renewal: Wild River Valley & Beyond*.

Dean Bennett
232 Bean Road
Mount Vernon, ME 04352
Phone: 207-293-2761
e-mail: dean.bennett@maine.edu

Other Books by J.H. Hall

Fiction
Cover Girl & Other Stories of Fly Fishermen in Maine
Paradise: Stories of a Changing Chesapeake

Nonfiction
Selling Fish: Stories from a Fishing Life
True Stories of Maine Fly Fishermen

CHESAPEAKE

REFLECTIONS

Stories from
VIRGINIA'S NORTHERN NECK

J.H. Hall

THE
History
PRESS

Published by The History Press
Charleston, SC 29403
www.historypress.net

First published 2009

Front cover images by Grayson Mattingly, Ditchley, Virginia. *Top*: Hal and his men.
Bottom: Peeler trap on Prentice Creek.
All images are from the Hall family collection unless otherwise noted.

"Paradise," "Otha's Ghost," "Close to Nature" and "Arrowheads" are works of fiction
and first appeared in *Paradise: Stories of a Changing Chesapeake* © Rappahannock Press
1994, 1995. "Croakers, Toads and Rock," "Uncle Harry's Funeral" and "Catch-and-
Release Gill Netting" first appeared in *Selling Fish* © Stackpole Books 2000.

ISBN 9781540234568

Library of Congress CIP data applied for.

For Preston, Evan and Brandon

CONTENTS

ACKNOWLEDGEMENTS

Special thanks to:
Ida C. Hall
Stephen and Jeanne Proctor
William H. Haynie
Grayson and Suzanne Mattingly
Dean and Sheila Bennett
Mary (Conway) Covington
Mack and M.J. Conway
Arthur Conway

BLUFF POINT, THE BIG PICTURE

One mild spring morning in 2003, my friend Pat and I gazed out onto the placid Chesapeake Bay from the southern end of Bluff Point, that precarious piece of land on the Western Shore of the Bay between Indian and Dividing Creeks. Seeing the place for the first time, Pat was struck by the sense of wildness and isolation that lay within a three-hour drive of Washington, D.C.

"It's beautiful," she said.

"It is," I said, "but I wish you could have seen it in the 1950s."

Before we left the beach, I made a perfunctory search for arrowheads in the tidal pools formed by the stubble of submerged marsh grass. In the past, these pools acted as collecting places for arrowheads, but lately the numbers of arrowheads and other artifacts had dropped sharply, most likely because the coastline known to Native Americans now lay somewhere in the Bay. But I looked anyway for old time's sake. Then we meandered back to where the two-track that connected the main road to the beach terminated. Recently, the main road had been raised and widened in order to accommodate the prospective buyers of the planned building lots.

There was a pickup truck sitting at the edge of the beach and two youngish-looking men sitting in the cab studying a map. We said hello and chatted for a while. They were friends and associates of the then owner of Bluff Point and had simply come to have a look at the property. It was very unusual to have so much undeveloped land so close to so many people, and they wanted to see it for themselves.

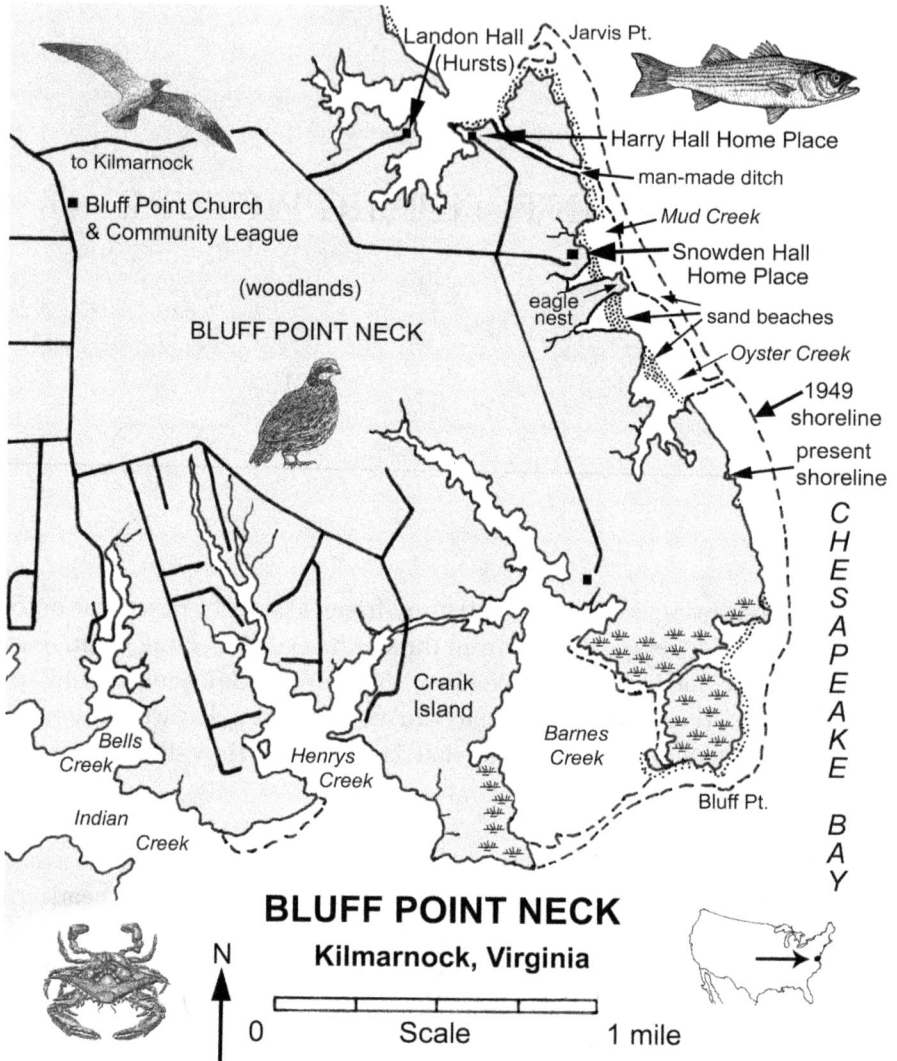

Landon Hall
(Hursts)
Jarvis Pt.

to Kilmarnock

■ Bluff Point Church
& Community League

Harry Hall Home Place

man-made ditch

Mud Creek

Snowden Hall
Home Place

(woodlands)

BLUFF POINT NECK

eagle
nest

sand beaches

Oyster Creek

1949
shoreline

present
shoreline

C
H
E
S
A
P
E
A
K
E

B
A
Y

Crank
Island

Barnes
Creek

Bells
Creek

Henrys
Creek

Indian
Creek

Bluff Pt.

BLUFF POINT NECK

N

Kilmarnock, Virginia

0   Scale   1 mile

Map by D.B.Bennett

I told them of my family's connection to that piece of land, how Uncle Eugene Hall had bought that land in 1943 and had contracted to sell it, but evidently before his death in 1960 changed his mind. However, he did not change his will, which made provisions for the "proceeds of the sale"; so the land was auctioned off. My father and his brother Ben attended the auction but found the asking price of $50,000 too steep for such low, wet land, most of which could not be farmed. Realistically, there were two building sites on which sat two fallen-in houses, abandoned for years, miles from the nearest power line. My father had his children's tuitions to pay; Ben had land of his own. So they let that piece go.

Hearing this story, the two men shook their heads sadly, knowingly. "They just didn't see the big picture," both men said, implying, of course, that they did see the "big picture." I said nothing. At the time I regretted the sale of the land out of the family, and I probably agreed with their assessment, but now, six years later, I am not so sure.

Now the "big picture" seems a rather elusive concept. For instance, how big a picture is worth seeing? Millions of years ago, the whole area was a seabed, as evidenced by the fossilized sharks' teeth and scallop shells found in the nearby woodlands. Five to ten thousand years ago, Native Americans inhabited the area, fishing and hunting with stone tools and cooking in clay pots. That way of life lasted until a few hundred years ago. Then the Europeans arrived. Surely the Native Americans must have believed that their way of life would last forever, and every generation of Native Americans was correct except the last. Some changes occur so slowly as to be imperceptible; others happen overnight.

For our purposes, we'll start in 1875, when the first Hall settled on Bluff Point. That would have been Private S.C. Hall of the Sixth Virginia Cavalry, who came to manage the lands of his friend and commanding officer, Colonel Richard H. Dulany of Loudoun County, Virginia. It is said that Private Hall dragged the wounded Dulany from a battlefield and saved his life. After the war, Colonel Dulany purchased 350 acres on Bluff Point Neck, but not the same acreage that Uncle Eugie later bought. Dulany bought the better land adjacent to the north that was bordered by Dividing Creek and the Bay. This was higher ground, suitable for farming, for building homes and, of course, for harboring boats that would harvest the Chesapeake's abundant fish, crabs and oysters.

But in those days, not everyone wanted to live in low, marshy land; malaria was still endemic to the area, and Dulany never lived on Bluff Point. Perhaps Private Hall was looking for a bit of peace and quiet after the war, in which he too had been seriously wounded. He took a Minié ball through the face, shattering his jaw and knocking out several teeth. A few inches higher and the shot would have killed him for sure, but he survived, and in 1875 moved with his son, Snowden, and daughters Nanny and Helen to Bluff Point to manage Dulany's land, where he built a house (since burned down) on the slender point of land that would later become the homeplace of Harry Hall. There, Snowden sired five more children: Daisy, Ethel, Ina, Harry and Eugene.

Snowden Hall homeplace.

Bluff Point Community League, formerly Bluff Point Graded School #3, recently added to the Virginia Landmarks Registry.

Though it was said that Private Hall and Colonel Dulany were friends before and after the Civil War, no written record of their relationship has been discovered, no letters or journals. However, we can surmise that the relationship was one of considerable affection, since four generations of Private Hall's descendants carried the "Dulany" name: his son Harry, Harry's son Hal, Hal's nephew Steve Proctor and Steve's daughter Shaune Colliver. Before he died, Colonel Dulany sold his Bluff Point land to Private Hall's sons, Harry and Snowden, for $4,000, the same amount he paid in 1875. The transfer of title was not complete until 1910, four years after Dulany's death, when his will was settled; so it is still not clear how much actual cash changed hands.

Snowden farmed and Harry fished, and in 1943, Eugene Hall, a bachelor, retired from school administrative work in West Virginia and returned home to live with Harry and Harry's wife, Gertrude. That same year, Eugie added the other piece of Bluff Point, as if completing the puzzle, consolidating the family holdings, creating for anyone who loved the out-of-doors (meaning most of our family) a virtual paradise of wildlife and privacy. I never knew my great-grandfather, but his offspring, their spouses and their offspring peopled this paradise of my childhood, and of my brother's and sister's and our cousin Steve's.

The memories of the physical place itself, its geographical features, are nearly as vivid as the memories of the people: two miles of bayshore with windblown pines, persimmon, pin oak, cactus, sea oats and other beach grasses, littered with intriguing flotsam, jetsam, pottery shards and arrowheads. Behind the beach lay the two brackish-water ponds, Mud and Oyster Creeks, which, though connected by a run, were distinctly different bodies of water. Mud Creek was shallower, fresher, with a soft bottom and, in the coves, dense vegetation. Puddle ducks loved Mud Creek, but it was not a place to fish. It was water that had to be traversed by rowboat to access the bayshore, which in those days lay several hundred yards away.

Oyster Creek was deeper, with a hard sand bottom, and by virtue of the "mouth" that periodically opened through the beach, Oyster Creek was saltier and more suitable for oysters. When the mouth was open, the fishing, particularly for gray perch, could be outstanding. Some of my fondest childhood memories are of Oyster Creek. It's where my brother and I, as very young children, caught our first fish from a rowboat with Uncle Carroll Hurst at the oars. Using heavy twine hand lines and hard crabs for bait, we practically filled the boat with perch but adamantly

Ida Hall behind the S.C. Hall homeplace, with Mud Creek, the Bayshore and the Chesapeake behind her, spring 1969. *Ida Hall photo.*

Looking across Mud Creek to Bayshore and its substantial vegetation, 1960s.

refused to stop fishing until the bait was gone, or so we, too young to remember, were often told by doting relatives.

Oyster Creek was appealing enough to diving ducks—golden-eye, Scaup and bufflehead—to justify the construction of a stake blind, from which it was well over a gun range to either shore, the beach to the east or Cedar Point and the woods to the west. In other words, it was a significant body of water and was separated from the Bay by a significant expanse of beach. One clear, very cold winter morning in the late 1950s, my cousin Steve and I hunted from that blind. The hunting was slow, and the cold was so penetrating that we built a fire on the wooden floor of the blind, fueled with the dried pine branches that camouflaged the structure. Why we didn't burn it down and ourselves up is a great mystery. Why no ducks decoyed to a blind that was billowing plumes of smoke is less mysterious. Now the bayshore lies somewhere on Cedar Point, and where that blind once stood is somewhere in the Bay; not a trace remains, not a piling or a plank. Who could have seen that coming? Who would have wanted to even if he could?

The author on the bayshore beside Oyster Creek in the early 1950s. Note the stake duck blind in left background.

Looking south across Jarvis Creek and the remains of Mud and Oyster Creeks, 1994. Note the ditch into Mud Creek. *Sherry Swan photo.*

Looking south across what is left of Mud and Oyster Creeks toward Bluff Point, 1994. *Sherry Swan photo.*

In 1960, all three Hall brothers of my grandfather's generation—Harry, Eugene and Snowden—died, and the place was never the same again. It was as if those three stalwart men, heroes of my childhood, served as anchors, not just of our family but of geography as well. Or perhaps it was simply that Snowden, Steve and I were coming of age, because it was another ten years before the commercial fishery failed and another twenty or so before the beach finally collapsed, but it seemed like it all began with the death of those men. Sometimes it is hard to document, or even acknowledge, changes as they happen, particularly unwelcome changes. We tend to divert our eyes or deny or see trends as natural cycles, which, of course, sometimes they are. But sometimes they are not; sometimes the pendulum does not swing back. Photographs can be helpful, and heartbreaking.

The photographic evidence shows that by 1994, most of Oyster Creek and much of Mud Creek was gone. Isolated coves remained and, though smaller, remain to this day, but the geographical integrity of both creeks was destroyed: there was no connecting run between them; the run and the portion of creeks it connected were in the Bay, as were most of the tall pines—the highest promontory on Bluff Point—that bordered the run. Eagles nest in those trees, but each year nest farther inland. Up and down the bayshore, pines have toppled like rows of soldiers into the Bay as the sea level, for whatever reason, rises, and the beaches, like an old man's hairline, slowly, and sometimes not so slowly, recede. No need to row across Mud Creek to reach the bayshore now; the beach has come to us. Only on Google Maps do both creeks, like ghosts, still exist. If only the satellite photos did not know and tell a different story.

Ironically, in the last half century the land that remained in our family has changed more than the land that left with Uncle Eugie's death. Though both have suffered equally at the hands of Mother Nature, nine new houses have gone up on our farm, but none on the other piece of Bluff Point. A larger road, yes, and drainage ditches, and some pines have been harvested, but in almost fifty years not one new house has been erected—probably for the same reasons my father and uncle did not tender an offer for the land in 1960; it is low, wet ground and shrinking. When surveyed in 1883, that piece of property measured 336 acres; a century later, the acreage was down to 298. Who knows what the future holds for Bluff Point?

Currently, the real estate market has fallen on hard times, almost unprecedented hard times. Perhaps the markets will rebound overnight and a new development will spring up next week. Perhaps the sea levels will fall and Mud and Oyster Creek will be reconstituted, bigger and better than

A 2009 photo from the bayshore beside the remnant of Oyster Creek.

ever. Who can say with any certainty? And how far into the future do we really want to see? It seems to me now that the "big picture" is never really clear except in retrospect, and maybe that is for the best.

UNCLE HARRY'S FUNERAL

When Steve and I first saw the fish, we were standing in Hal's yard reminiscing about Harry Hall, my great-uncle, Steve's grandfather, whose funeral was that same afternoon.

It was spring, and the birdsongs, the warm air, the scent of fresh grass, jonquils and forsythia cast a spell on us. The herring had already run; the first peeler crabs had moved inshore to shed, attracting striped bass to the shallows in search of the succulent soft crabs—which probably accounted for the occasional flashes of silver. A school of stripers—"rock"—had evidently moved into the grassy cove back of Hal's house, which until two days ago had been Uncle Harry's house. Now it was all Hal's—the farm, the fishing boats, the crab floats, wharf and oyster-shore that lay inside the Sand Point, where it now appeared that fish were feeding.

Steve and I meandered toward the shoreline for a better look. A gull dove. We shielded our eyes, studied the situation and came to the same conclusion: yep, it was a school of rock all right. Wasn't that something? Fresh from the city, with a funeral to attend, we were not in our "fishing mode." We were still in our city clothes—slacks, sport shirts and street shoes. Sometimes as young adults you just had to accept the fact that there would be times when it was not appropriate to go fishing, even when, as it now appeared, fish were feeding practically at your doorstep. So we stood at the edge of the yard in the warm, late morning sunshine and reminisced about Harry Hall. Wasn't it ironic, we agreed, that all three Hall brothers died in the same year, 1960, and that Harry, the frailest and not the youngest, outlived both of his brothers, Eugie and Snowden.

Left to right: Harry Hall, Ray Kesby and Eugene Hall aboard the *Mary Virginia* in the early 1950s.

There were several surviving daughters, but those were the only sons of the "original" Snowden Hall, who had managed the farm of Colonel Richard Dulany, whose life Hall had saved in the Civil War. This was the place that, no matter how much it eroded or how far we wandered from it, would always feel most like home to our family.

My favorite recollections of Harry were the times when he, Eugie and Hal would come and visit at my grandparents' house after a holiday meal, usually Thanksgiving or Christmas. Those three would sit on the sofa in the crowded little dining room while the rest of us finished eating. Talk would always turn to hunting, fishing, oystering or crabbing, and usually the men would end up arguing about some seemingly minor detail, such as which way the wind had been blowing that morning at Deep Hole when they caught $5,000 worth of croaker. Or how many bushels of oysters Hal had nippered up six winters ago; or how many ducks they might have killed on another morning and how many of which species. But these seemingly minor details were never insignificant to them, and weather was never small talk to a waterman.

As I recall, Harry never lost an argument. Hal's memory, for a variety of reasons, wasn't the best even then, and Uncle Eugie, though the best educated of the men—almost a PhD—was not the contentious type. But Harry could be quite cantankerous, and his jimmy-jaw gave him a feisty, defiant look that seemed to define him. He had a thick shock of black hair that did not turn gray until his very last years. Harry's son Hal had the same hair, but his turned gray much sooner, possibly as a result of being Harry's son.

Harry was a tough taskmaster, a hard man to please. Even when his heart was failing and he was too weak to fish, he continued going out with Hal on the *Mary Virginia* to "supervise" almost up until the day he died. Rain or shine, rough seas or calm, in sickness and in health, come sunup, sometimes sooner, Harry Hall was onboard the *Mary Virginia*. And he was still in charge, still captain. Even when he was too short of breath to walk from the house to the dock without stopping to rest, he could still give orders: tighten up that line; tow that skiff closer astern; get that fish slime off the gunnel before somebody slips up and falls overboard! What's the matter with you, boy? Hal was in his thirties then, had been fishing his entire life and needed no supervision, but I never heard him talk back or once lose his temper.

While Steve and I were reminiscing, a few more gulls had moved onto the flats. It was not a feeding frenzy by any means, but the activity was accelerating enough to make us nervous. The tide was so high that the cove seemed about to overflow its banks and spill onto the lawn. There was obvious evidence of fish feeding just beneath the surface: small fish skittering across the water, fleeing; gulls hovering expectantly; a subtle flash of silver and the occasional intriguing swirl of a significant fish. The cove seemed ready to boil over at any minute. It was enough to make any fisherman's mouth water.

"Too bad we've got to go to that funeral," I said.

"Yeah, it sure is," Steve said.

"Of course, it's only eleven o'clock," I said, looking at my watch. The funeral wasn't until two.

Steve restlessly scraped the dirt with the toe of his shoe. It had to be his decision. Harry was "only" my great-uncle; he was Steve's grandfather. Closest of kin had to make the call.

"I doubt Granddad would be offended if we went fishing on the day of his funeral," Steve said.

"I wouldn't think so either."

Steve was and is a nice man. Strange to say, he went on to become a lawyer, but even in those days his arguments were persuasive. He very promptly convinced me that we did not just have a right to go after those fish; we had

Hal Hall on his way to work, circa 1968.

an obligation. Otherwise we would be letting Harry Hall down, maybe the whole family. After a few minutes of listening to Steve, I was a bit ashamed that it had taken us so long to discern Harry's wishes. He wanted us to get after those fish. In fact, he was probably put out with us for standing around and wasting so much time. Soon the tide would change and we would have missed our chance. "You boys call yourselves fishermen?" we could hear him say. "You call yourselves Halls? What a trifling lot!"

It did not take us long to assemble our gear. There was a spinning rod in Steve's car and another in the dock shed. We did not bother changing clothes. So what if we got a few fish scales on our good shoes? So what if we came to Harry's funeral smelling like fish? What could be more appropriate? Harry probably smelled like fish himself. It would take more than a little formaldehyde to flush the fish out of Harry's system. As long as any portion of Harry Hall existed, on earth or in heaven, whatever form he took—flesh and blood or spirit—fish would be a part of him.

There was no question of us sneaking out onto the creek sight unseen. Jarvis Creek was like an arena, its shores dotted with houses, many belonging to family members. By the time of the funeral, our fishing activities were known to all. However, as if to prove that we had read the signs correctly, not one person suggested that we had done anything wrong or disrespectful by fishing right up until a few minutes before the actual services. All anyone wanted to know was how the fishing was. (It was fine.)What had we caught? (More than a dozen school-sized rock.) What did we use for bait? (Spoons.) What was the tide? And, of course, what was the direction of the wind?

PARADISE

At first light, Roy Simon was already up and on his way to his uncle's house. If you were going to be a commercial fisherman, you had to get up early. You couldn't lie around in bed all day like some people he knew.

The dirt road passed like a valley between two fields of corn. The stalks, some twice as tall as Roy, rustled in the light breeze. A quail whistled from the hedgerow. Roy whistled back, off-key, silencing the quail. "Awright," Roy said. "If that's how you're going to be, I'll see you in November." His family would be back for Thanksgiving, and he and his uncle, Lester Harmon, would hunt birds together. Then at Christmas they would hunt ducks and geese. His father did not hunt or fish. He sold real estate and played golf.

Last night there had been an argument about golf. It was a short argument. Roy didn't even like his father to bring his golf clubs to the country, but his father liked to practice sand-irons on the bayshore. The bayshore was a sanctuary, wild, with no houses. You could walk for two miles and see nothing but washed-up bottles, crab pot buoys and arrowheads. Once Roy had his picture in the *Richmond Times* with his arrowhead collection. He had tried to teach his father the names of the arrowheads—Halifax, Lamoka, Morrow Mountain—but it was hopeless. How could you teach something like that to a person who saw the bayshore as a big sand trap?

Lester lived alone on a narrow peninsula in a white frame house flanked by a pair of silver maples, whose limbs overhung the tin roof like protective arms. Roy stood in the yard and looked around at the cove and the crab

floats; at Lester's dock and big boat, the *Mary V*; at the white skiffs lying still in the water; and, to the east, at the creek and the beach and beyond the beach out into the Bay, which seemed vast and endless. "This place is paradise," Roy said. "Why can't he see it?" Sometimes his father would walk around the place, using his hands as a viewfinder. Roy knew exactly what he was doing. He was measuring house lots.

Roy heard a noise, turned and saw his father's Buick station wagon pull into the yard. His father, Rud, was a large man with pinkish skin that would not tan and thinning silvery hair. He walked over to Roy. "I'm still not playing golf," Roy said.

"You made that clear last night," his father said. His father looked around, his eyes adjusting to the dim light. "So," he said, "I thought, if you didn't mind, and if it was all right with Lester, I would go out fishing with you. With Lester."

"Oh," Roy said.

"If you don't think Lester would mind."

"No. No, I'm sure he wouldn't mind."

They walked down to the dock, where Lester and his hired man, Otha, were readying the boat. Roy's father was wearing white Bermuda shorts, a baby blue golf shirt and a pair of dark glasses dangling from his neck. Roy was wearing blue jeans, a T-shirt and tennis shoes. No dark glasses for Roy. Dark glasses were for city people, "come-hithers." Watermen, like Lester, didn't wear dark glasses; they wore baseball caps, and they squinted. Squinting was what caused the creases in the corners of their eyes that turned white when their faces relaxed. Lester's face was lined and furrowed like soft leather, like Roy's baseball glove. Otha's face was black and round as a catcher's mitt. Otha had worked for Lester longer than Roy had been alive.

Otha was loading boxes and barrels into the bow of the *Mary V* when Roy and his father walked out onto the dock. Lester was tinkering with the engine. They were both wearing olive green oilskins and baseball caps. "Uh oh, Cap'n," Otha said when he saw who was coming, "looks like we got a full crew today."

Lester looked up from the engine box. "Darned if we don't."

"I won't be in your way, will I?" Rud asked.

"No, indeed," Lester said. "Glad to have you. Can't pay much, though."

Roy laughed.

"He's telling the truth now," Otha said. "He don't pay anybody much."

"That's the trouble with people these days," Lester said. "They all want to make big money, but they don't want to work." Lester hit the ignition, and Otha's comeback was lost in the roar of the engine. Roy laughed anyway. He was sure that whatever Otha said would have been funny. He thought Otha and Lester were two of the most comical men he had ever known. He thought they should have been on TV.

"They're right funny, aren't they?" Roy said to his father. He had to shout to be heard over the engine.

His father nodded and patted his shirt pocket. "I wish I'd thought to bring my Dramamine," he said.

"What?"

"I wish I'd brought my Dramamine."

Roy shook his head. "Calm as it is, you won't need it today."

Lester throttled back, shifted gears and eased the boat out into the channel. "It's a Gray Marine," Roy said. "First V-8 on the creek."

"Is that a fact?" Rud said.

Roy lay on top of the small forward cabin and watched the sunrise. The Bay was as smooth as thermometer mercury, motionless except for the groundswells that moved through the water like a large animal under a blanket. The slow rolling motion almost rocked Roy to sleep, but his father sat rigidly upright, his hands fastened to the rim of the deck like claws. With every swell, he pushed up as if riding a horse. Roy reached over and touched his father's arm. "Just relax," he said. "Don't fight it."

"Right," Rud said.

Roy wished his father hadn't come. These things never worked. Once he had tried to show his father how to read and break peeler crabs, and his father somehow managed to get both his thumbs crushed. Roy still wasn't sure exactly how it happened. One minute his father had the crab safely by the back fins; the next minute the crab had him by the thumbs. His father howled in pain, and Roy—like a fool, he knew, but it was before he realized how much it hurt—laughed. He hadn't meant to, but it all happened so fast it was like magic, like sleight of hand. Another time he had tried to show his father how to shuck an oyster and the oyster ended up in small pieces, with the oyster knife stuck into the palm of his father's hand. At least that time Roy didn't laugh.

Lester and Otha tied the big boat to the pound net stakes, climbed over into the skiff they'd towed out and paddled around to the top of the net. Lester leaned over, pulled up a line and lashed it to a stake. "That's the anchor line to the pound net," Roy said. "And that one holds the funnel between the false pound and the pound open."

His father nodded and swallowed.

Lester shoved the top line of a loose section of net underwater with the oar and in the same motion slid the skiff over the net. "Did you see that?" Roy said, but his father was looking the other way.

Lester and Otha paddled to the far side of the pound and worked a slack piece of net up so that all the fish were between them and the big boat, but still deep and out of sight. As they pulled themselves toward the *Mary V*, Roy moved to the edge of the deck. "This is the good part," he said. "This is where it gets exciting."

"I think I'll go sit up there for a while," his father said, pointing to the very bow.

"What?"

"I think I'll feel better if I can see the land."

"But you'll miss the best part."

"I'm sorry. It can't be helped." His father went and sat on the bow and stared inland at the beach and the trees and the fields. Roy watched him for a moment and then turned away and watched the fishing.

As Lester and Otha tightened the net, the trapped fish became increasingly frantic. Small fish drove their noses through the mesh. Larger fish shimmied up the sides of the net. Fish leaped into the air. They churned the water to a froth.

"A few spot," Lester said as he and Otha slacked the net to settle the fish.

"How many boxes you think you got?" Roy asked.

"Hard to tell," Lester said. "We got a few though."

Roy shook his head. He'd bet anything that Lester had those fish sorted, weighed and sold already and that he knew the price to the nearest dollar.

Lester looked up from the fish for a moment, removed his cap and wiped his forehead with his arm. "Is your father all right?"

"Yeah, he's fine," Roy said. "He just wanted to see the farm from another angle. You know how these real estate people are." Roy was glad when Lester started bailing fish, because Roy did not want to talk about his father. The less said about his father the better. Roy did not want to be the son of someone who got seasick.

While Otha bailed the undersized fish and sea nettles overboard, Lester bailed the good fish into the *Mary V.* The first netfuls of fish made a hollow drumming sound against the floorboards. Then, as fish piled on fish, there was a flat drumming sound, and a fine mist of fish slime and seawater rose a foot or so above the fish. Then the drumming quieted and the mist disappeared as the fish settled, their gills flared, colors darkened and their markings became more distinct: the deep gold of the spot; the dark green along the backs of the bluefish that turned silver along the belly; the mottled brown and silver of the gray trout and croaker; the sharp black spots of the speckled trout; the mother-of-pearl sides of the butterfish. But they weren't all beautiful. The oyster toad's head looked like it had been stepped on; its lower jaw jutted out like a drawer full of teeth. Its brown, slimy skin bristled with spines. The swell-toads were more foolish looking than ugly, with their headlight eyes and rabbit teeth and habit of inflating themselves with air so that in the boat they'd lie around like volleyballs. If space became a problem, a pocket knife was the solution.

When Lester finished bailing fish, he climbed back into the big boat and rolled a barrel on its edge over to the gunnel. When he stood the barrel upright, fish squirted out from under it like spit watermelon seeds. He started sorting the crabs that Otha handed up one netful at a time. "Are you sure your father's all right?"

"Oh, yeah, he's fine," Roy said.

"I think if it was my father, I might want to go and check on him."

Roy did not want to check on his father, but since Lester had asked, what could he do? Lester was the captain of that boat, and the captain had absolute authority. So Roy said, "All right," and slowly, reluctantly, moved up and sat beside his father.

"So how you doing?" Roy asked.

His father shrugged noncommittally. His skin was the color of seawater.

"No better, huh?"

His father shook his head and swallowed.

"You're not going to get sick, are you?"

His father swallowed again.

"Damn—I mean darn. I hope you don't get sick. You think you can hold it 'til we get back?"

His father sighed.

"The other nets are hung up drying," Roy said. "This is the only net we're going to fish today. Thirty, forty minutes at the most and we'll be back on shore."

"Thank God," his father said through a narrow slit.

"That bad, huh? I'll tell you what, we'll make a deal. If you don't get sick, when we get back, we'll go play golf. I mean it. As soon as we get back, we'll go over to the bayshore. Okay?"

His father looked at him, his eyes glazed and weary. "Please leave me alone," he said. Then his mouth clamped shut like an oyster.

"Okay, okay, I'm leaving. I wouldn't have bothered you in the first place except Lester made me." He patted his father on the leg. "I hope you feel better."

Roy scooted back to where he'd been sitting. Lester shook a large jimmy crab off the end of his heavy rubber glove into a bushel basket and then dumped the sooks and smaller males, all connected by their claws, into the barrel. "So how's your father doing?" Lester asked.

"Well," Roy said. "I guess he is a little under the weather. We've all had a touch of the flu. He had it worse'n any of us. I thought he was over it, but I guess not. He'll be all right, though. He'll shake it off. I'm telling you, these Simons are tough. They're almost as tough as Harmons."

Then his father leaned out over the bow as far as he could and vomited profusely for several minutes.

"Damn flu bug," Roy said. "I knew he shouldn't have come. And he shouldn't have drunk all that beer last night either, tired as he was from driving. I've never seen a man could drink so much beer."

His father sat up, wiped his face with his handkerchief, blew his nose and took a few deep breaths. "I do not have the flu," he announced in a raspy voice. "And I am not hung over. I am seasick. Is that such a crime?"

"Jesus Christ!" Roy thought.

"Well, is it?"

"No, indeed," Lester said. "If it was, there'd be some watermen right here on this creek that would be in jail. Isn't that right, Otha?"

"Yes, my Lord," Otha said. "Cap'n Jimmy, he'd be doing life."

"Jimmy Gaskins?" Roy asked.

"He gets sick every time he goes out," Lester said. "Least that's what they tell me."

"I never heard that before," Roy said.

"It's the truth," Otha said. "He goes down below, does what he has to do and then comes back up and goes right on about his business."

"Otha knows, too," Lester said. "He used to work for him."

"That I did. Worked seven winters drudging oysters all the way up to the Potomac River."

"Otha's not real loyal," Lester said. "He'll work for anybody that pays him enough."

"And some that don't," Otha said.

Rud moved down and sat beside his son. "Usually I take Dramamine," he said. "But I left in such a hurry this morning, I forgot it. If I don't take it, just like clockwork. Something about those swells."

"That's just the way it was with Cap'n Jimmy," Otha said. "He didn't mind a rough sea much as he did a groundswell. Just exactly the same. He might even be a kin of yours."

"No, all my people are from inland."

"I'd of never known that," Otha said. "I'd of taken you for a Guineaman myself. Wouldn't you, Cap'n Les?"

"Either that or a Tangierman," Lester said.

"No, my Lawd," Otha said. "Got too much sense to be a Tangierman. And he talks too plain."

"I guess if I had much sense, I'd have stayed onshore."

"You can't keep a Guineaman onshore," Otha said. "Any waterman, he got to be on the water."

"I'm no waterman," Rud said.

"Got to be a little bit," Otha said. "Any man come out knowing he going to get sick, he's got to love the water. Ain't that right?"

"Darn right," Lester said. "He's got to love it more'n I do, I'll tell you that. I couldn't do it. I'd have to get me an office job in the city, with a big desk and a nice young secretary to take care of me."

"Now you talking," Otha said, handing up a netful of crabs. "Now you saying something. It would be goodbye, Mr. Sea Nettle, you done stung me the last time."

Lester laughed. "What'd the preacher say, Otha?"

"Preacher? He say, 'My, my, those are nice tomatoes.'"

They both laughed at the private joke.

"And what did Wheeler say?"

"He say, 'Slow'er down, Cheetum. Slow'er down.'"

They both laughed again, and this time Roy's father laughed with them, as if he too understood the joke, but Roy, who knew all about the wino, Wheeler, and the preacher who mooched tomatoes (and fish and crabs—whatever was in season), did not laugh. He sat quietly and stared off at the different colored crab pot buoys that dotted the Bay like decorations, and at the crab potters, moving slowly along the strings of pots. There was C.E. Lee in the *Jean*, and Junior Boy Willis, who used his wife to pull his pots by hand long after the others had gone to mechanical winders. And there was Jeter Jenkins, who couldn't talk plain, and Crittenden Campbell in the *Three Kids*, only now there were just two, because one had suffocated trying to keep warm in the small cabin one cold day when his father was oystering back of the marshes.

Roy could recognize them all even from half a mile away: the *Jean* by the way her bow rose straight up out of the water—she had the most deadrise on the creek—and Junior Boy Willis's wife by the way she stayed hunched over even when she wasn't pulling pots, and Jeter Jenkins by his big belly, and Crittenden Campbell by the way he rocked back and forth at the tiller. Roy knew them all, and they knew him, and they would talk to him when they pulled alongside the *Mary V* for bait, the boats sometimes three deep, and the men, even in rough weather, walking gunnel to engine box to gunnel as easily as other men might walk down the street. They wouldn't talk to him like he was a "come-hither" either. They talked to him like he belonged, like he was one of them, because they knew that Roy knew the fish and the boats and the water. He knew the Bay. And now his father, who didn't know anything, didn't know how to dress or how to talk or how to act, was being treated like a big hero—by Otha and Lester, of all people! For what? For puking overboard, as if that was some great accomplishment, like knowing how to read a peeler or shuck an oyster or recognize a boat from half a mile away.

"You feel all right?" his father said. "You're awfully quiet."

"Yeah, I feel fine," Roy said.

"You sure? You've been so quiet."

"Don't worry about it, okay?"

"I hope you're not getting it too. Maybe it runs in the family."

"No," Roy said. "It does not run in the family. Not in the Harmon family, anyway."

His father stared at him. They were both quiet now. Now everybody was quiet except Otha, who had started humming this gospel, spiritual-type hymn that Roy hated. That was one thing about Otha; when the going got rough, he would sometimes slip into this Uncle Remus character just for safekeeping. Lester could disappoint you too, but at least he didn't hum.

"Well, I hope you feel all right," his father finally said. Then, turning away, "I certainly feel a lot better."

"You look like you do," Lester said. "Your color's a whole lot better."

"That's just how it was with Cap'n Jimmy," Otha said. "He got sick, but he didn't stay sick."

Roy wished that Otha would shut up about Jimmy Gaskins. Roy knew Jimmy Gaskins. Many a day he'd sat with binoculars and watched Jimmy Gaskins bring his boat back into the creek. Jimmy would stand there with his head cocked back and little cap tipped low over his eyes to shield them from the setting sun, one hand tucked behind his oilskin apron and the other on the wheel. He'd dock that big boat—it was close to seventy feet—with two swishes of its tail. It had twin screws; he could turn it on a dime. When he hit the throttle that last time, just before he killed the engine, you could hear the rumble all the way across the creek.

Roy rode back lying on the bow. The sun bore down on him and salt spray flew into his face. A flock of gulls dove in the wake for scraps of fish, and a pair of ospreys peered over the edge of their nest on the black beacon. By the time they got back to the dock, Roy felt better. The Bay always did that. It was like a medicine. For some people.

Roy walked his father back to the car. He said he was sorry that he talked like he did. He didn't know what got into him sometimes. His father said not to worry about it; it didn't matter. At least now he knew where he belonged.

"You did all right," Roy said. "They thought so."

"Well, that's what counts, isn't it?" Rud said. Then he smiled.

Roy couldn't tell if his father was serious or not. That happened a lot.

"Well, I'm going to hit some golf balls," his father said. "You can come if you like, but don't feel obligated."

"I guess I'll hang around and help Lester and Otha sort fish," Roy said.

"Okay."

Roy watched his father walk across the lawn to his car. He seemed surprisingly spry. Roy waited until the car disappeared up the lane. Then he walked back down to the dock. He put on a pair of short rubber boots and rubber gloves and slid down into the *Mary V.* Otha and Lester were tossing fish into boxes and baskets. Their hands moved so fast that fish were always in the air. Roy scooped up three spot and tossed them into a bushel basket.

"Your father seems to be feeling better," Lester said.

"I guess he is," Roy said. "He's gone off to hit some golf balls."

Lester stood up and stretched his back. "Now there's a game I never could quite understand. Must be something to it, though, as many people as play it. But darned if I could figure it out. Could you, Otha?"

"No, my Lord. I wouldn't know one end of a golf ball from the other."

"Me either," Lester said.

"That makes three of us," Roy said.

Roy liked wading around in the fish. He liked the weight of the fish on his boots and the feel of them in his hands. He even liked how they smelled. Only city people thought fish stunk. He liked everything about the place, but what he liked best was working alongside Lester and Otha, listening to their banter. They were good people, the best, and if they sometimes went a little too far in trying to make an outsider feel at home, well, you couldn't hold that against them. That's just how they were.

"That was nice what you did for my father," Roy said.

"What's that?" Lester said, tossing a big gray trout into a basket.

"That business about Jimmy Gaskins."

"We didn't do anything for your father."

"That man does for himself," Otha said.

Well, naturally they weren't going to admit it to him, but Roy knew for a fact—he'd bet anything—that Jimmy Gaskins had never been seasick a day in his life.

CROAKERS, TOADS AND ROCK

In our family album, there is a faded black-and-white photo taken aboard the work boat *Mary Virginia* in the early 1950s. In the foreground, I am holding a "jumbo" hardhead, also known as a "croaker," that must have weighed four or five pounds.

In the background, Hal stands on the stern working the tiller with his foot. Uncle Harry, jimmy-jawed, already frail, stares pensively into the water. Walter Schwab, married to Harry's sister Ina, is, like me, along for the ride. He sits on the gunnel staring at the camera. I am smiling because I am happy, because for that one radiant moment all the ingredients of my childhood happiness are in place: my feet are firmly planted in a pile of fish, my hands are holding a fish and I am on the Chesapeake with Harry and Hal.

A croaker is called that because it makes a deep croaking noise, and it's called hardhead because—no surprise here—it has a very hard head with exceedingly sharp gill plates that make handling them without gloves tricky, especially removing one from a gill net. By either name, they were for years one of the most valuable fish on the Bay. Their firm, white meat made excellent table fare and did not spoil as fast as the softer spot or trout. Harry and Hal's most lucrative fishing ever came from a huge haul of croaker from the Deep Hole trap before my time, but I heard the story more than once—$5,000 fishing!—and never tired of hearing it.

Croakers are also good sport on hook and line; they're bottom feeders that bite readily and pull hard. They are a ruggedly handsome fish as well,

The author with a jumbo hardhead on the *Mary Virginia*, circa 1952. *Others, left to right*: Harry Hall, Hal Hall and Walter Schwab. Note the swelltoads in the lower left corner.

somewhat resembling a redfish, but not as sleek. All in all, there is nothing not to like about a croaker, but when their numbers crashed, there was no great outcry from commercial or sport fishermen. Sport fishing was not a big industry then, and commercial fishermen knew that fish populations always ran in cycles. When one species declined, another often flourished. Spot and croaker seemed to have a reciprocal relationship, their populations seesawing back and forth in tandem.

A few years later, the numbers of swelltoads, also known as blowfish, dropped, and once again, hardly anyone seemed to notice. The only person I ever heard lament the decline of swelltoads was a man known as "Lappa Dick," a slightly tongue-tied fish buyer at Little Bay, where Hal sold his catch. One hot summer day in the early sixties, Lappa Dick, out of frustration, asked when Hal was going to "bwing me anudder load a toads?"

Hal laughed, not because of how Lappa Dick talked—Hal would never have done that—but because Lappa Dick sounded irritated, as if Hal had some control over what species swam into his nets and, by not catching toads, was simply being contrary.

S.C. Hall (actually Jr.) spoils his grandsons, circa 1946. *Left to right*: Snowden III (actually IV) and the author.

Except for that conversation, I doubt that I would have noticed either that the toads' numbers were down. Swelltoads are funny-looking fish that you are not apt to see mounted on anyone's wall. They're boxy, with gnarly brown- and yellow-splotched sides, bug-eyes and rabbit-like front teeth. They will take bait but do not fight much. They just twitch at the end of the line as if more puzzled by the hook than seriously upset. Skinned and served as something else such as "Chicken of the Sea," they are said to be delicious, though personally I have never tried one. But nonetheless, swelltoads were always a special fish for me, because my grandfather could and did blow them up like balloons, or so I believed at the time.

When my brother Snowden and I were tykes, we would pester our poor grandfather to take us fishing—"deep-sea fishing" we called it, meaning we wanted to go to the Bay and not into Oyster Creek. So he would take us out to the "Middle Ground" or the "Narrows," two somewhat vague locations in Dividing Creek, where we would bottom-fish with hand lines of thick twine, our hooks baited with hunks of hard crab. It was neither elegant nor particularly sporting, but it was as much fun as I've ever had fishing.

When we caught a swelltoad, our grandfather would hold it to his mouth, placing his lips just behind the pectoral fin, and huff and puff, and the fish's white, sandpaper-textured belly would fill with air until the fish was no more than a leathery white ball with bug-eyes, buck teeth and a twitchy little tail. I would laugh and granddaddy would toss the toad overboard, where it would instantly deflate and slowly swim away, none the worse for wear. To this day, I do not know if it is actually possible to inflate a swelltoad this way—I have my doubts—but I do know that they will inflate themselves if you tickle their bellies or simply hold them out of the water for a while. I suppose it is a protective mechanism. (But what is the point when they are already out of the water? Seems a bit late then.)

And then, rather abruptly, the toads disappeared. There was no great hue and cry, no "Protect the Toads" T-shirts, no demands for shorter seasons or tighter limits. Except for Lappa Dick's plaintive remark, there was nothing but silence, and perhaps a sigh of relief from Hal's hired hands who had to do the skinning for, to my knowledge, no extra pay.

But a few years later, the striped bass numbers plummeted, and all hell broke loose. Because striped bass, known locally as "rock," are not a funny-looking fish. They are silvery and sleek, with elegant black lines down each side like racing stripes. At times they feed on the surface on schools of menhaden beneath flocks of frenzied, screaming, diving gulls. And they will take artificial lures—spoons, bucktails, rubber eels and flies—and therefore

Same cast of characters, different watermelon, on the steps of the old kitchen at the Snowden Hall homeplace.

are a favorite of sport fishermen, who had come to think of stripers as their own private species, no matter that commercial fishermen liked them too.

The striped bass's dense white meat is delectable. In our family, rock was a "baking fish," a high compliment shared with buck shad, gray trout and practically no other species. A load of striped bass always brought a high price. The fact was that everybody liked striped bass, and in those not too distant, but seemingly innocent, days, most people admired commercial fishermen too. Their independent spirit, their rich traditions and quaint ways, their lore and language inspired numerous books. Museums commemorated the tools of their trade and the various styles of their handsome, functional boats.

However, when the striped bass mysteriously disappeared, commercial fishermen suddenly went from role models to villains, as if it was all their fault. Even if commercial fishing was one factor in the stripers' decline, it was certainly not the only one, or likely the largest. I knew from personal experience how much commercial fishermen loved the Bay and everything that lived therein. For them to be criticized by newly minted conservationists in the form of sport fishermen seemed grossly unfair. It still seems unfair.

The first conservationist I ever saw in action on the Chesapeake was Otha, a large black man who worked for Hal for many years. While Hal and his other helper would bail the good fish, those large enough to sell, into the *Mary Virginia*, Otha would bail the small fish overboard. He would even free the fish that got trapped along the gunnel, including the lowly chokefish, which in the old days was trotline bait but currently was of no "use" to anyone. And the chokefish were not easy to pick up; they're flat like a small flounder and would adhere to the gunnel like placemats. But Otha, sometimes using his fingernails, would patiently lift each one and toss it over. I never asked why. The gentle way he handled them, handled every fish, seemed answer enough.

I do not believe that Otha would have understood that to some people he was an enemy of the Bay. For that matter, I doubt that he would have liked me calling him a "conservationist" either. He was a waterman, plain and simple, as were Uncle Harry, Hal and sometimes Eugie. Being a waterman did not need to be defended, because it was not a crime. As Hal, who could get quite religious at times, used to remind us, no less than four of Jesus' disciples were commercial fishermen.

More recently, the striped bass have made something of a comeback. The reasons are no clearer than the reasons for their disappearance. Reduced pollution, stricter limits or even natural cycles may all have played a role. Small croaker are also showing signs of a recovery. No word yet on the humble swelltoad, but their resurgence is not likely to make headlines anyway.

WHEN THE WORLD WAS
MINE OYSTER

It is said that oysters are an aphrodisiac, but in our family they had a different effect: they made us dig ditches. It was not consuming oysters that did it, but dreaming of them and the fortunes to be made in their cultivation. Oysters were the fool's gold of commercial fishing.

The first so afflicted was Uncle Goldsborough Hall, my great-grandfather's brother, who, in the late 1800s, ditched from Barnes Creek at the end of Bluff Point to the Chesapeake at Henry's Creek. (According to one unconfirmed version of the story, he worked with recently freed slaves.) He left no written record, but there could have been but one motive: oysters. Barnes Creek was landlocked and brackish. Adding the Bay's salinity would potentially transform Barnes Creek into a sheltered sanctuary for raising oysters, safe from the vagaries of tides, weather and other oystermen. Whether this actually came to pass or not, we do not know. Barnes Creek, as such, barely exists today, though the ditch lives on as a permanent waterway crossed by a substantial bridge connecting the mainland to what is now called Bayberry Island (née Crank Island). If there was a lesson in this story, if indeed it was a cautionary tale, it went unheeded by most of our family.

In the 1950s, a ditch was dug through Harry Hall's bay field, and the only dissenting voice on record was that of Harry's daughter Eleanor, who warned that the ditch would "ruin that field" where she and her sister Winnie owned lots. The men prevailed. Land was cheap, and any damage would surely be more than offset by the fortune made raising oysters in Oyster Creek. The creek's very name—derived from the few, but huge, oysters that grew wild along its shore—was a mandate to dig, and the half measures had already failed: the wooden culvert meant to keep the natural mouth across the bayshore open had repeatedly sanded over. There was no other choice: it was either outflank the beach with an end run through the field or ignore the very destiny of Oyster Creek.

In those days, no environmental impact statement was required. All you needed was a steam shovel. When the ditch was completed, we youngsters could and did jump across it. It was a fascinating new playground with a reversible tidal current with crabs swimming to and fro, and sometimes snakes. (Back then, catching snakes was a form of entertainment ranked below fishing, firecrackers and looking for arrowheads, but still in our top five.) Unnoticed by us at the time, each tide carried a bit of the ditch's soft side walls with it; slowly but surely, the channel widened. Apparently, this was part of the plan.

By 1964, the ditch was wide enough to allow the passage of a skiff and deep enough at high tide to float a scow filled with seed oysters through the ditch and through Mud Creek to its destination in Oyster Creek. It took careful timing; the tide needed to be high enough to float the scow but still rising. A falling tide would create such a current in the ditch that a skiff towing a scow laden with oysters could make no headway. If the tide had not risen sufficiently, the skiff would run aground in the head of Mud Creek, where the soft bottom would not allow anyone to wade and push. The water was shallow, but the mud was evidently bottomless and remarkably soft, so soft, in fact—and this was the solution—that the outboard engine could plow through it without jeopardizing prop or shear pin, leaving a wake of black goo. Ahead lay Oyster Creek, an oasis of deep water and hard sand bottom—a paradise for oysters.

The summer of 1964 was like no other in my life. I had just finished college up north and had not yet started medical school. My sister Ida was fourteen. We both spent the summer on Bluff Point. Ida stayed with Ben and Louise; I stayed at the old homeplace alone, though I took my meals with them. In the mornings, Ida went trap fishing with Hal, while I helped Ben dredge seed oysters in Jarvis Creek in his twenty-foot work boat. Ben was an elementary school principal with the summer off. He worked hard but would not be hurried, which was why I liked working with him. Each day had its own pleasant, leisurely rhythm. In the mornings, before the heat was too severe, we would do the dredging, cull the seed, shovel them into the scow and cover them with a canvas tarp. In the afternoon or evening, when the tide was rising, we would make our trip to Oyster Creek.

The halcyon days of the 1960s. *Left to right*: Louise, Ben and Ida Hall and Rusty Acree aboard the sailboat that Ben crafted very carefully over several years. *Ida Hall photo.*

Between the dredging and the tide would come lunch, not a snack, but a full-course meal—fried chicken, deviled crab or leftover beef— that would leave me lethargic and drowsy. So I would usually make an excuse to visit the other house, where I would fall asleep on the glider on the screened porch, not a sound to be heard but songbirds, quail, a breeze rustling through cornstalks or the distant Bay lapping against the beach. I'd awaken in time for our trip to Oyster Creek, where, if we were running late, we'd leave the scow and unload the seed the next day. Some evenings I spent with Susan, a local beauty Louise had introduced me to. I even played a little golf on the unpretentious little course just down the road at Indian Creek.

Away from Bluff Point, the world was not quite so tranquil. It was the time of social turmoil, racial strife and civil rights. Virginia was much in the news, and at college in New Jersey I was often confronted by my classmates on matters of race; heated arguments often ensued. I tried to explain, "It's not as simple as you think," but to them it was as simple as black and white. To me, it was infinitely complex. For instance, how was I to explain the relationship between my blind grandmother and

Becalmed, 1964. *Ida Hall photo.*

Linda Johnson, an ageless black woman, who was my grandmother's nearly constant companion in her later years? Yes, Linda cooked and she might have even done a little cleaning, but she was so much more than a paid employee and so much less than a member of the family. That sort of quasi-intimacy between blacks and whites has become a Hollywood cliché, but before it was a cliché, and after, it was a reality, and a complicated one at that.

One inviolable part of Linda's and grandmother's routine was their "stories," the afternoon soap operas, which they diligently watched together in the little sitting room. From the living room, I could overhear their running commentary on the characters. Grandmother had a tiny sliver of peripheral vision and would sit sideways to the TV, and sometimes Linda would have to explain the onscreen action, and Linda would often editorialize: "Ain't she awful!" And from grandmother would come a sort of rueful clucking or "tsk-tsking" at the terrible behavior of these licentious city people, whose terrible behavior somehow held them both spellbound for hours. If you hadn't known better, you might have thought you were eavesdropping on a conversation between equals, which it was not, I realize, but what it was exactly was hard to explain.

And how was I supposed to explain my Uncle Ben, the kindest, most generous man I ever met? I never saw him treat anyone of either race with anything but the utmost respect and consideration. He was, in the truest and best sense of the word, a gentleman. And yet, I know that he too struggled with the issue of race. He once asked how I would feel if my sister Ida were to marry a black man. I don't recall my exact answer but do recall that it did not satisfy him.

That was the same school year that, according to a newspaper report, Ben turned away a small group of black children who attempted to integrate his elementary school in White Stone. I say "according to a newspaper account" because that was the only account I had or ever would have. Evidently, a few parents brought their children to his school, and Ben advised them to "Go on home," or words to that effect, and they turned and went on home. No fire hoses, no police dogs, just a quiet word from Ben, and the incident, such as it was, ended. But, of course, being a recent college graduate and naturally curious—and nosy too—I wanted to know more. That summer, I kept waiting for Ben to bring it up, but he never mentioned it. Finally, foolishly, one hot afternoon in Oyster Creek, I asked him.

We were shoveling seed along the shoreline near Cedar Point. All we could see from where we worked was water, beach, woods and a corner of one field. All we could hear were sounds of oysters hitting the water, waves upon the beach and the screech of a seagull or osprey. There were no houses in sight, no cars, no roads, no phones, and we would have had to cross a sizable expanse of beach even to see another boat. It was a portrait of tranquility and isolation, a world away from that other, somewhat unreal world we would see on television or read about in newspapers. If only I had left it like that.

Periodically, Ben would pause to mop his brow with his handkerchief or shirt sleeve, to brush away a mosquito or simply to look around at the creek. It was during one such pause that I asked my question. "What was it that actually happened at your school with those black kids?" I asked. "The paper didn't give many details."

Ben's face turned redder than could be explained by the heat of the afternoon, and he never said a word, not then, not ever on that particular subject, and I never asked again and wished I hadn't asked that time. Ben may have been the kindest, most generous man I ever met, but obviously there were things about him that I did not comprehend. And how could I hope to explain racial relationships in the South to my northern classmates when I did not even understand the ones in my own family?

Ben died in 1975, outliving his mother by a mere five years. I don't know if he ever made a dime from those oysters. Certainly it was never the windfall anyone imagined. After Ben died, Hal harvested and sold a few for Louise, but that was about the last we heard of those oysters until the late 1990s, when my sister received a report that someone—looked like a black man, probably a deer hunter—had been seen walking the shores of Oyster Creek, and he appeared to be picking up oysters. By that time, the beach was mostly gone, and a waterman working in the Bay could look directly into Oyster Creek, and a waterman made the report.

Halls and Hursts did not hunt deer; they hunted quail and waterfowl. But other than grandmother ("It's a sin to kill a deer"), we had no quarrel with deer hunters. The most prominent local ones belonged to the Ditchley Hunt Club, a group of African American men who leased and hunted what was then the Chesapeake Corporation woodlands adjacent to our farm. We had a cordial relationship with them, and that year, in exchange for a favor, Ida had given the Ditchley Hunt Club permission to hunt the farm, much of which she now owned outright. So it was not surprising that a black man might have been seen along the edge of Oyster Creek, and as for the oysters, they were welcome to them. By then there were not enough to worry about, and Ida often shared fish with area blacks, many of whom she knew personally, and they probably knew she wouldn't mind. For all the hunters knew, the oysters might have been growing wild.

But later, when she told me this, I had to laugh. What irony! Those oysters were very likely either left over from, or the progeny of, the seed that Ben and I had planted that wonderful summer of 1964. Suppose Ben had known then that those oysters we were sweating over would be harvested by blacks, possibly even some of the same children who had attempted to integrate his school? What would his reaction have been to that? My guess is that he would have mopped his brow, chuckled and kept right on shoveling. As reluctant as he might have been to accept certain social changes, I am certain that he would not have begrudged those men, black or white, a single oyster.

Now, in 2009, Oyster Creek hardly exists, oysters have basically disappeared and we have an African American in the White House. I'm not implying cause and effect, only pointing out that some of the seemingly most permanent fixtures of our youth—geographic or social—can be amazingly insubstantial. In a few short decades, they can be swept away by the winds and tides of change—quite literally, in the case of the beach. Even in 1964, it was fairly clear that segregation of the races would be short-lived, but I

Natural strike of wild oysters in Jarvis Creek, 2009.

More wild oysters from Jarvis Creek, 2009. Not all are dying young. The teaspoon is for scale only; these oysters were not eaten.

never expected the oysters to up and die. Dermo? MSX? I had never even heard of them. And, most of all, I was absolutely certain—I took it for granted—that Mud and Oyster Creeks would be there forever, and I could not have been more mistaken.

OTHA'S GHOST

Lester Harmon did not consider himself a racist, not by any means, but he had to admit that some colored people sorely tested his patience, and none tested it more severely than Otha Lee Taylor.

For fifteen years, Lester had worked side by side with Otha, driving stakes, tarring and hanging nets, bailing fish, sorting crabs, sweating in the hot August sun, shivering in March rains. They'd shared secrets and they'd argued and they'd suffered one another's long, stony silences. Over the years, Lester had come to trust Otha and rely on him. Then, one December, despite Lester's warnings, Otha went back to dredging oysters up near the Potomac River, fell overboard and drowned.

They knew what day he drowned; it was cold but not rough. The dredge hung on the bottom and tipped the boat far over to one side. Before the captain could release the clutch, the dredge pulled free, and the boat rocked hard the other way. Otha lost his balance and went overboard. They knew who the captain was. He was a good man. That made it Otha's fault.

"If he could have stayed afloat two minutes, that boat could have swung around and picked him up," Lester said.

"Right hard to swim in oilskins," said C.E. Lee, Lester's friend and fellow waterman.

"You'd think a man who spent as much time on the water as Otha did could swim a stroke or two."

"That cold water probably stunned him."

"Two minutes!"

Lester and C.E. Lee were the only white people at Otha's funeral. They were not altogether sober, but they were there. After the service, Otha's widow, Hattie, came up and comforted Lester for his loss. "He just worked for me," Lester said. "That's all."

Afterward, Lester didn't feel quite right about that remark, but what was he supposed to say? C.E. Lee was there, and Lester was embarrassed. And Otha wasn't family, and he wasn't really a friend. Whites didn't have colored friends. Otha worked for him; he was an employee. No, there was more to it than that, but he didn't know what you called it.

In the spring, Lester hired three different men to take Otha's place. Not one lasted longer than a week. The first one drank too much. The second didn't drink but didn't work much either, and the third, Albert, talked constantly. He didn't talk about normal things either, such as fish and crabs and other watermen; he talked about "civil rights." That was the last thing Lester wanted to hear about. He didn't even know what they were. When Lester let

Albert go, he told him he'd be better off—they all would be—if he spent less time worrying about civil rights and more time learning how to swim.

After that, Lester tried to fish the *Mary V* alone. Fishing alone was not easy. It was a lot of work for one man. It was wearing Lester down. He wasn't sleeping well, either. He was having bad dreams about Otha—his eyes sad and accusing, teeth shining like tombstones, lips round and rubbery as an inner tube, or a life preserver, which if a man couldn't swim, he ought to keep nearby, if he had any sense. That sort of carelessness made Lester angry. There was no excuse for it. "I'd like to see to him one more time just to tell him how mad at him I am."

He sort of missed him too. He missed arguing with him while they fished the traps. It had helped pass the time of day. Otha had liked to argue. He'd been good at it, too. He read, and he kept up on things. In some ways, he'd been a right smart man. In other ways not so smart, because it wasn't too smart to argue too well with the man you worked for, and sometimes Otha would sort of out-argue Lester, but not anymore. Now he lost every argument. Lester tried to be fair about it too. He'd been around Otha so long, he knew how his mind worked, and he could pretty much imagine what Otha would have said in any situation. Lester did his best to fairly represent Otha's side of the argument, but Lester's side was always just a little more convincing. Lester won about sixteen arguments in a row. He supposed he should have known that, dead or alive, Otha wouldn't tolerate that for long.

One day, as Lester was fishing his traps and putting the finishing touches on his latest victory, he heard a humming sound. At first he thought it was the wind or the bowline rubbing on a trap stake, or even a croaker grumbling underwater. But none of those could carry a tune, and Otha could. He was humming "That Old Rugged Cross," one of his favorites. Lester liked it too. He never told Otha, but he could always work a little harder when Otha was humming one of his gospels.

"I always did like that song," Lester said, when Otha was done. "'That Old Rugged Cross, a symbol of suffering and shame.'"

"Yes, suh, that's what it is, suffrin and shame, suffrin and shame."

Otha's voice sounded perfectly normal, deep, soft and gravelly.

"You sound all right," Lester said.

"Can't complain, can't complain, considering the circumstances," Otha said. "And how 'bout you, Cap'n? You doing all right?"

"About fair," Lester said. "Working right hard and not sleeping so well. Too hot to sleep, I guess."

"Something troublin' your mind, I'd say."

Lester put the dip net down. "Well, to tell you the truth, I've been a little put out with you."

"With me?" Otha asked, sounding hurt and innocent.

"Hire out to another man, go off and get yourself drowned, leave me without any help, leave your family like that—that's no way to act."

"No need to take it personal."

"Maybe not, but I sort of did anyway. I'd gotten right used to you."

"Well, Cap'n, you know there's two ways of looking at that. For instance, if you paid a man a living wage, he wouldn't have to hire out in winter."

"I paid you all right."

"All right nine years ago. Not one raise since."

"You never asked for one."

"Not a day went by I didn't ask for one, one way or another."

"I thought you were fooling with me."

"Course you did, 'cause that's what you wanted to think."

"Are you blaming me for what happened?"

"Naw, suh, I'm not blaming you. I'm just saying what's what."

"It sounds to me like you're saying if I'd paid you more, you wouldn't have drowned."

"I said no such thing."

"You might as well have."

"But I didn't."

This was upsetting Lester. He'd forgotten how sneaky Otha was. He didn't argue fair. He had a way of twisting words around, a way of getting *you* to say what was on *his* mind. Before Lester could figure out what to say, C.E. Lee pulled alongside in his boat to buy crab bait.

"What are you talking to yourself so much about?" C.E. said, tying the two boats gunnel to gunnel.

"Who said I was talking to myself?"

"Lips moving a mile a minute. Didn't even hear my engine."

"Not that it's any of your business, but I was talking to Otha Lee."

"Oh, Lord. Did he talk back?"

"Suppose I said he did?"

"Wouldn't be too surprised. Take more'n a drowning to shut that Negra up. You got any big bunkers? I don't want any more of those little ones that fall right out of the bait bag. Save those for Jeter."

"I'll look," Lester said, "soon as I finish bailing these fish."

That was the last he mentioned Otha. C.E. Lee didn't believe in the spirit world. Only spirits he believed in came out of a bottle, and Lester didn't feel like being laughed at. So he dropped the subject, sold his bait and said goodbye. But he was still troubled by his conversation with Otha. "Imagine Otha blaming me, after all I did for him."

That night, Lester didn't sleep well. He was afraid to sleep. Several times he'd doze off and then catch himself and jerk awake. He smoked a cigarette; he almost never smoked in bed. Soon he got up, dressed, went downstairs and had a cup of coffee and a slice of dry toast. Then he walked down to the dock.

Otha was sitting on the gunnel drinking ice water out of a Mason jar, same as always. He looked a little pale, and his skin was puckered, the way it gets after you stay in the tub too long, but otherwise, he looked all right. Lester had seen him look worse. Lester spoke first.

"I've been thinking about what you said."

"What's that, Cap'n?"

"I don't think you're being fair complaining about how I paid you. Maybe I didn't exactly give you a raise, but I gave you a bonus every Christmas."

"'Preciate it too, 'deed I do. Bought myself a bottle of wine every year and change left over."

"And any time we had extra good fishing, I paid you extra."

"Yes suh, I expect you did. Way I remember it, I worked extra too."

"I didn't have to pay you extra. I just did it out of the goodness of my heart."

"Yes suh, I understand that."

"So?" Lester thought he'd given a pretty good account of himself.

"I never said you weren't a good man, Mr. Harmon. You treated me better'n most white people treat colored around here."

"Darn right I did." Looked like another victory for Lester.

"Just the same, there's still a lot of hungry mouths to feed up my way."

"Well," Lester said, "you should have thought about that before you went off and got yourself drowned."

"I did. It's why I went."

This was getting nowhere. They were talking in circles. "What do you want from me anyway?" Lester said. "Why are you here? Why are you harassing me?"

Otha said nothing. He just looked at Lester. His eyes were huge, sad and accusing, same as in the dream. Otha picked up a mop and began washing down the gunnel and humming "Onward Christian Soldiers."

"Don't start that humming," Lester said. "I don't want to hear any humming now."

"Don't work for you no more. Hums when I feel like it."

"Gotten right uppity, haven't you?"

"Don't mean to be." He kept on scrubbing, leaning into a place where a dead fish had gotten ground into the gunnel. "You're not keeping this boat clean like you ought to."

"She fishes just as well clean or dirty," Lester said. This was an old argument; he didn't want to get into this again.

"Right much boat for one man anyhow."

"Well, maybe I'll get some help."

"Haven't so far."

"I still might. You don't know. You don't know everything. You just think you do."

"Time you were slowing down anyway, Cap'n. You're getting on in years."

"Not that old."

"Naw suh, not that young either."

"What are you driving at anyway?" Lester didn't like the drift of this conversation.

"Big work boat like this'd bring a nice price. Nigh 'bout $2,000, I'd say."

"It's not for sale."

"$2,000'd do a lot of good for my people."

Lester couldn't believe what he was hearing. "You want me to sell this boat and give the money to your family!?"

"Now that's an idea," Otha said. "Might help you sleep better too. Maybe we'd both rest easier knowing my family was cared for."

"That's blackmail!" Lester said.

"Naw suh, I'd say it's more like back wages. Don't come to much more'n $200 a year. That's not even a dollar a day raise. Don't sound like much to me."

"I never heard of such a thing!" Lester said. "In all my life." Lester was pacing back and forth on the dock.

"Well, don't do it if you don't feel like doing it," Otha said. "It's altogether up to you." Then Otha resumed humming "Onward Christian Soldiers," a very spirited version with a sort of martial beat. He shouldered the mop like a rifle and marched into the little cabin in the bow of the *Mary V*.

"Come back here," Lester said. "I'm not done talking to you yet." But Otha was gone, and Lester wasn't about to go into that cabin after him either. "Darn Negra!" Lester said.

It was about the most aggravating thing that had ever happened to Lester. Not seeing Otha's ghost. He half expected that. If you believed the

Spirit of Jesus Christ was still alive in the world, as Lester did about half the time (his faith ran a fever curve: struck like malaria, departed in a cold chill), then it wasn't hard to believe in other spirits. What got Lester was, this spirit was blackmailing him, this man he'd trusted and tried to do right by. "Is this what they mean by 'civil rights?'" Lester said. "Playing tricks on white people?"

The next day, there were no fish in his Deep Hole net, not a one. Something had cut a big hole in the pound, and all the fish had escaped. Lester had never seen such a thing. "What the dickens?" he said. The only thing that could cut a net like that was a big shark, but there weren't any big sharks in the Chesapeake Bay. Well, occasionally a bull shark would wander in from the ocean, strangle itself in a gill net and get its picture in the *Rappahannock Record*. So Lester decided that must have been what happened, but the whole time he was mending net, he was cursing Otha.

On the way in, his engine conked out. He'd had engine trouble before, plenty of it, but he'd never had it cut out with no warning. "Must be the gas line," Lester said.

It was. It had come apart right in the center. He'd never see that happen before. He used to keep an extra piece of tubing in the cabin. He looked but he couldn't find it. He didn't look long, though. It was hot and stuffy in the cabin, and messy—dirty rags, pieces of rope, spare wrenches and there was a hornets' nest in one corner, with hornets in it. Also, the place was haunted.

Lester sat on the bow in the hot sun and smoked a cigarette. There was no breeze and the tide was slack, so he wasn't going anywhere. He just sat and smoked one cigarette after another and waited. "Hope you're happy now," he said, but Otha wasn't answering anymore. Lester had a strange feeling he wouldn't be seeing Otha again, only his good works: broken gas lines and empty nets. He felt a cold chill, cold and familiar.

Soon C.E. Lee pulled alongside, as Lester had known eventually he would.

"What the heck you doing?" C.E. asked.

"Just passing the time of day," Lester said.

"I see that."

"Got anything I can use for a gas line?"

"No indeed."

"Then I guess you'll have to give me a tow."

"I guess I will."

While they were rigging up the lines, Lester asked if C.E. knew anybody looking for a used work boat.

"You're talking foolish now," C.E. said.

"Too much work for one man," Lester said. "Too much aggravation."

"Get some help."

"That's even more aggravation."

"There was a fellow from Reedville," C.E. said, straightening up, stretching his back. "A crab potter, asking about a boat." He gave Lester the man's name.

"Maybe I'll give him a call," Lester said.

"Then what?"

"Might do some gilling out of my skiff. Catch about as many food fish as I would in a trap anyway."

"Might, but what am I supposed to do for crab bait? You're the last trap fisherman on the creek."

"Buy frozen bait."

"I don't believe in frozen bait. Doesn't catch like fresh."

"I can't solve my problems and yours too," Lester said.

"Oughtn't to talk like that to a man who's about to tow you in."

"Don't guess I should."

"Might cut this line and set you adrift."

"Wouldn't be the first time that happened."

That same evening, Lester called the man from Reedville, and bright and early the next morning he was there to look at the boat.

"She's solid as a rock," Lester said. "She's just too much for me. I've gotten a little too feeble to fish her anymore." He bent over and limped around as he showed the boat.

He didn't mention Otha's ghost. No need to. The man didn't ask. If the man had asked if the boat was haunted, Lester wouldn't have lied. He would have said, yes, she was, a little bit in the cabin. The rest of her was all right. But the man never asked.

The day after he got paid, Lester carried twenty crisp $100 bills in an envelope to Otha's widow, Hattie, a frail, elderly woman in a light cotton dress. She met Lester outside her trailer and led him over to the sparse shade of a flowering mimosa. Otha's grandchildren played on the bare ground around them.

"How you doing this day, Mr. Harmon?" Hattie asked. She sounded genuinely concerned.

"Doing about fair," Lester said. "I brought you something."

"I see you did."

He handed her the envelope. She peeked inside and then quickly shut the envelope and looked away.

"Now I don't want you getting overly excited about this," Lester said. He'd heard Otha speak of his wife's weak heart many a time, suspected it was a play for sympathy, but now he wasn't sure. "It's just some money I owed your husband."

"More'n 'some' money."

"$2,000," Lester said.

"Oh, my Lord," Hattie said, patting her chest.

Lester pulled a lawn chair into the shade and eased Hattie into it. Then he sat down beside her. "Now you put this money in the bank," Lester said. "You have a bank account?"

"Do now."

"Use it for necessities. Don't let the young ones get their hands on it. Fact, I wouldn't even mention it to them."

She shook her head. "No, my Lord. They'd throw it away."

"Probably be best if you didn't mention it to anybody. Just let it be our secret." The fewer people who knew about this, the better.

"Yes indeed, that's just what it is, our secret. Not anybody else's. And wouldn't anybody have know'ed if you hadn't paid this money either. You're a good man, Mr. Harmon. Lord knows, you are, and I thanks you."

"Well, I wanted to do what was right," Lester said. "Otha was a right good fellow."

"'Deed he was, and I know you miss him too."

"In some ways I guess I do," Lester said.

Lester was chuckling as he walked back to his truck. It felt good to give that money away, but that's not why he was chuckling. He was chuckling because the joke was on Otha. Otha knew a lot about many things, but he didn't know much about the value of a good work boat. The fact was, Lester didn't sell it for $2,000. He sold it for $4,500. He made more off the deal than Otha did. "And that Negra thought he was so smart," Lester said.

A BRIEF HISTORY OF QUAIL
HUNTING ON BLUFF POINT

For anyone who has never hunted quail or even heard their haunting call, it is no doubt difficult to comprehend the power that such a simple two-note whistle—bobwhite—exerts upon some of us. Like Proust's madeleines, that call evokes another time; it casts a spell. That quail song was as much the acoustical background of my youth as was the pop music of the day, and far more powerful. Even now.

Once, years after my youth, on a quiet, still evening on a small bass pond in central Maine, I heard the unmistakable call of a quail from a nearby meadow and then an answering call from a wooded hillside. An unsettling anomaly: quail do not live within five hundred miles of Maine, but these were unquestionably quail. On that pond I commonly heard loons, ducks, geese, eagles, osprey but never quail. They are ground feeders and cannot survive Maine winters…unless. Was it possible that global warming, about which so much had been written, had expanded the quail's range? No, it was not. I realized and later confirmed that these were pen-raised quail kept for dog training. But even knowing that, I could not help noticing that time and distance had not diluted the powerful effect of their call.

My most vivid Christmas memories as a child are not of any present—not a bicycle, BB gun or train set—but of our traditional Christmas breakfast of quail, grits and that concentrated essence of the bird, its nectar—quail gravy. Not only were quail magical, but their delicate, white meat was the gold standard of poultry, the perfection that ducks, geese, chicken, turkey, pheasant, even—its closest rival—grouse could never quite attain.

And in the field, quail were the perfect quarry: difficult but fair. It takes but a few shots to bring one down, but to get oneself in position to put those few shots in contact with a quail takes luck, timing and teamwork—between man and dog—but most of all, sadly, it requires quail in numbers sufficient to justify a hunter owning a dog and taking the time to train him and the trouble to hunt him.

I killed my first quail on our Bluff Point farm in the late 1950s in a windrow my Uncle Ben had created by clearing a field in front of his new house. I had to fight my father's English setter Jack for the bird, but it was my first quail, and I would not be denied even if it meant shoving my hand halfway down the dog's throat, which it did.

I killed my last quail on a nearby hunting preserve in the late 1990s. It had been pen raised and released that very morning, its approximate location marked with a small red pennant. It just so happened that my personal hunting history coincided with the decline—let's not say "demise" quite yet—of quail hunting in Virginia. Let's hope someone else's hunting history will coincide with quail's recovery, but it clearly will not be mine. There have been ups and downs in quail populations before, but never anything so well documented and that looks so definitive as the devastation of the last half century.

According to family lore, great-Uncle Carroll Hurst used to bird hunt from his home at Landon Hall all the way to Kilmarnock and back wearing hip boots. The story was as remarkable for the footwear—hip boots not being good hiking shoes—as for the amount of accessible hunting territory and the number of quail the story implied.

That was well before my time, but as recently as the 1970s on our farm alone, there were about a dozen coveys. That did not mean that finding them was easy. Some days you could hunt the entire farm and never see or hear a bird, because quail are capable of vanishing acts beyond the ken of even the most competent, cooperative bird dog, much less the rangy, cantankerous brutes we usually hunted. When the birds do not move to feed, they leave no scent and are virtually undetectable by dog or man, unless by chance you practically step on them, at which point they explode with such shocking suddenness and noise that getting off any shot, much less an accurate one, is unlikely.

My father was a doctor and dedicated bird hunter who lived in Danville, Virginia. He had access to excellent hunting territory in Pittsylvania County courtesy of grateful patients such as William Newell and J.L. Link, but more than once he said, "Acre for acre, I think there're more birds on Bluff Point

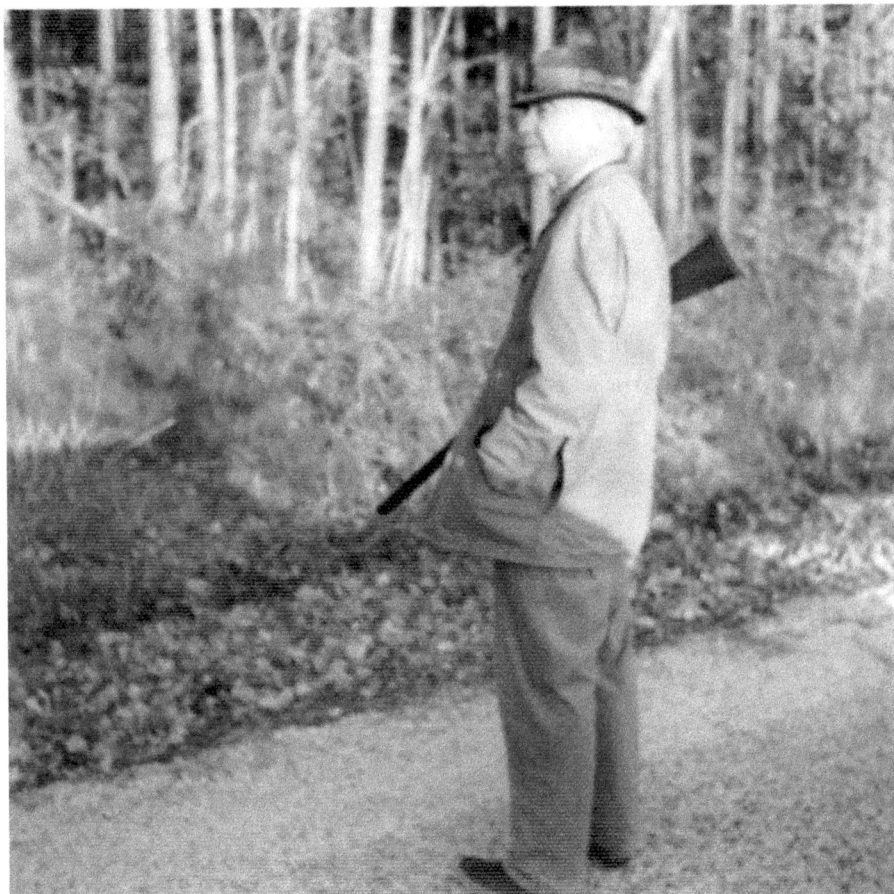

Ben Hall in hunting garb, 1960s.

than any other place I hunt." Unfortunately, his hunting time on Bluff Point was limited to Thanksgiving and Christmas holidays. His brother Benjamin, however, lived his entire life on that Bluff Point farm and had the time, but for most of his life he simply lacked the inclination to hunt birds. He was not a hunter or a fisherman; he was a gardener, an orchardist and a builder. He could grow, make or fix anything. For years he cured his own hams. So why, one day in 1964, he decided to buy a female pointer was somewhat of a mystery, since it was clearly not to hunt her, and another breed might have made a better pet. Or might not have. Quite likely, any animal raised as Ben and his wife Louise raised Sweetie Pie (for, sadly, that was the name they saddled her with) would have made a superb pet.

Ben and his beloved Sweetie Pie (I).

Sweetie Pie had the run of the house; she slept on the sofa or almost anywhere else she chose to sleep. My brother, my father and I were appalled—by her name as much as by her treatment. Female bird dogs were traditionally called Lady, Belle or Queenie—something distinguished and preferably southern, but never anything so sugary as Sweetie Pie. Likewise, bird dogs did not belong in the house and certainly did not sleep on a sofa. They slept outside on the hard bare ground or in a Spartan, unheated doghouse. Real bird dogs were not meant to be pets; they were professional athletes. They were not put on earth to be loved but to be trained—preferably by another professional—and if at the completion of that training they performed well in the field, they were petted and praised, but they still rode home in the trunk of the car. (Once Mike and Tony rode all the way to Georgia in the trunk and did not seem to mind it one bit. We said, "Load up!" and they hopped in, curled up and went to sleep, and arrived none the worse for the experience.) The point is, bird dogs were accustomed to rough treatment; they expected it, and we believed it was for their own good. We were not alone in our thinking. An illustrative digression:

After my first year of medical school, I worked in a surgical lab with experimental animals, to what purpose I forget, but this I remember clearly: most of the animals were bird dogs, and each dog was X-rayed, and every bird dog without exception carried birdshot in its rump. That was what became of rangy, unruly bird dogs, the hard cases. Before the advent of electric collars, shooting an overly rangy dog from a safe distance was an accepted training method: you yelled "Whoa!" to a running dog, and if they did not stop, you fired. Either the dog would put two and two together or they were donated to science. I'm sure that most of my father's dogs carried birdshot in their haunches—I put some there myself—but they were never donated to science. They went to good homes. So in that way my father was kinder than the average owner of bird dogs of the time. He gave one beautiful, gun-shy setter, Hector, to his mother. He gave a frivolous, fun-loving Gordon setter, Judge, my sister's pet (but a trifling bird dog), to the yardman, John Henry. And he gave his rangiest, most recalcitrant of all, Snowboy, a gorgeous, pure-white English setter, to me, because I naively believed that I could cure the dog of running off. Where on earth did I get such an idea? I got it from Uncle Ben and Sweetie Pie, that's where.

I watched Ben spoil this dog for years. The worst he ever disciplined her was—usually to impress one of us—when he threatened to get the flyswatter. On those rare occasions when he actually touched it to her backside—perhaps to remove her from "unapproved" furniture—it was done so gently and with such affection that the blow would not have hurt a fly, much less a dog, and yet the gesture did its job. Sweetie was such a sensitive animal and so attuned to her owner's desires that she understood the flyswatter was meant as a reprimand. She even knew the word, so that eventually all Ben ever had to do was mention "flyswatter" and the dog would slink guiltily off the forbidden furniture and onto the floor.

And then, when Sweetie was well into her middle years, Ben decided that she ought to be hunted. Occasionally, Ben would ask me to take her out, but it never quite suited. I was away most of the time at school, and frankly the idea of summoning a hunting dog with a cry of "Here, Sweetie!" seemed to undermine the manly enterprise that hunting was supposed to be. Eventually, Ben took matters into his own hands: he took her hunting.

He and Sweetie never killed a single bird, not one. Needless to say, Ben blamed his poor shooting and not the dog, because it went without saying that the dog was flawless. "She did fine," he said. "She found birds. She pointed the birds. I couldn't hit the side of a barn." Ben, who died in 1975, was an exceedingly kind man. He treated us like his children. For me not to have taken his dog hunting when the opportunity arose would have been an act of terrible ingratitude. So one day I took her and, indeed, she was flawless. With the possible exception of her successor, she was the best bird dog in our family in my lifetime. I hunted them all, and I know.

I don't recall the precise details of that first hunt with Sweetie, because they have blended into the memories of many more hunts, which I recall as a single, sun-splashed fall afternoon, with an abundance of quail and an obedient, well-behaved dog. It was a new experience hunting a dog like Sweetie, a relief and a rare treat to work with such a tractable animal. She was nowhere near as rangy as the male dogs my father owned, but ranginess is a mixed blessing. With Sweetie, I did not have to wonder constantly where she was or how many birds she had found and flushed on her own. She would even turn to check in with me from time to time; she was oriented as much to the hunter as to the birds—a novel concept among Hall dogs.

Her nose was excellent, and when she found birds, which was often in those days, she did not charge recklessly in, as her male counterparts were prone to do. She moved step by step; she let you flush the birds, and she was diligent in search of dead birds. Unlike some dogs (Tony), she did not make a perfunctory search for downed birds and then run off chasing singles. She also did not eat birds (unlike Jack), and she did not bite (unlike Sam); sometimes she even retrieved (unlike every other dog we ever owned)! We did not expect field trial performances from our dogs. We asked only a modicum of competence and cooperation and, except for Sweetie, rarely received it. More often, our kindest overtures were met with pigheadedness or outright delinquency. Probably our overtures came too late, after rigorous, professional training—bird dog boot camp—but who had time or the ability to train a bird dog? Sweetie never received that training. She seemed merely to enjoy hunting quail and pleasing people

Sweetie Pies I and II at rest, circa 1974.

in equal measure. It was hard not to draw conclusions or turn a dog story into a parable—which was what led me, in 1973, to take Snowboy off my father's hands. Love and kindness would no doubt turn this wild, beautiful English setter into a devoted servant. It was not to be. One night, a few years later in Maine, he ran off foraging for chickens (we know it was chickens, because he had already killed and left us a small barred Rock hen) and was never seen again.

My most intensive year of quail hunting came in 1972 on Bluff Point. I was just back from the West Coast, unemployed, confused about the past and future—a difficult year during which the only points of stability were, depending on the season, a gill net and a shotgun. I hunted almost every day that bird season. Some days I hunted alone with Sweetie, but when Hal was available and was not oystering or pursuing ducks with Steve, I hunted with him and his slightly demented male pointer Sam, a serious hunting animal with a serious personality disorder—but, amazingly, a littermate to Sweetie Pie. Once he literally hijacked Hal's car. Of course, the dog couldn't go anywhere, but neither could anyone else as long as Sam sat in the driver's seat snarling at anyone, even Hal, who dared to approach. There was nothing to do but wait him out.

Sam did not eat birds, but he did not always surrender them willingly either. He bit Hal once (and paid for it with a beating) when Hal tried to remove a bird from his mouth before the dog was ready to relinquish it, and he bit Charles Ball once for no apparent reason other than that the calf of Charles's leg was available. They were not even hunting. But Sam never bit me, because I never gave him the chance. I never hunted him without Hal; I doubt the dog would have gone, and I know I wouldn't have.

That year, Hal and I usually hunted on the farm or on Chesapeake Corporation land, but our best day came on Crank Island, a small island named, it is said, for the "cranky" brothers who lived on it. It only became an island in the late 1800s when Uncle Goldsborough Hall dug a ditch from Barnes Creek to an inlet of the Bay. So there was a family connection. There were only a couple of coveys on Crank Island, but one winter afternoon Hal and I scattered them both in the marsh beside Goldsborough's ditch. The ground was soft and the tall grasses were either pushed over or clumped up such that the quail could not run. They had no choice but to hold, as one by one Sam located and pointed nine consecutive single birds. When he wasn't biting someone or hijacking cars, Sam was a splendid bird dog: he had great instincts, a good nose and he was steady on point. That day he was perfect and so were we: we downed all nine birds. Many times in the next three decades, Hal would recall with great fondness, same as he recalled hunting and fishing stories from before my time, that day on Crank Island when we killed nine single birds in a row. "And Sam pointed every one of them," he would always add. "He was a right good dog at times."

Now, except on the older maps, Crank Island is called Bayberry Island—sounds better, I suppose—and hard beside the marsh where we scattered those birds, well within gun range, stands a handsome new home.

In 1974, with Sweetie in her declining years, Ben bought another female liver and white pointer from the same friend and neighbor, Jack Enoch, from

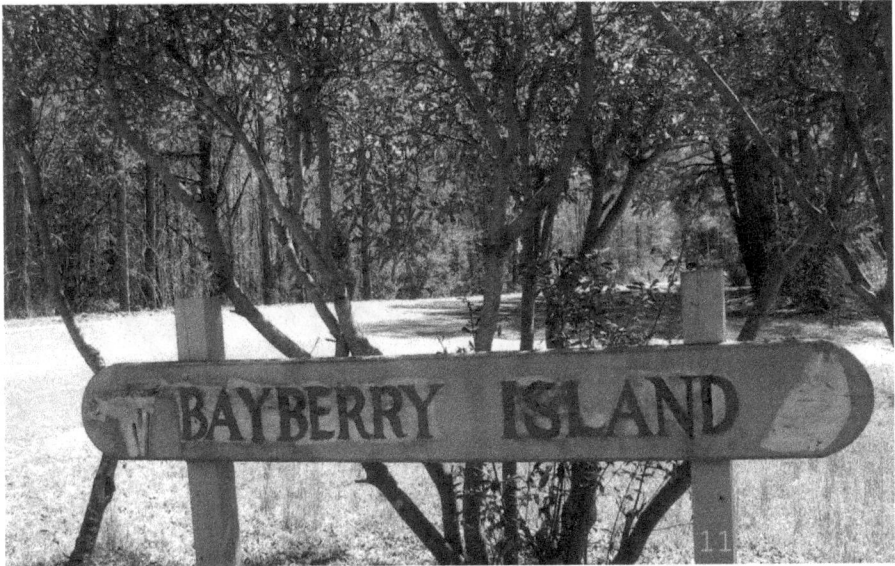

Crank Island, renamed, 2009.

whom he had bought Sweetie. They named this one Sweetie Pie also, but to avoid confusion they called her Pie. Sweetie and Pie, but this time nobody laughed. If anything, Pie was even better than her predecessor, faster, leaner and slightly more elegant on point. But the comparison may be unfair, since Sweetie was beyond her prime when she first hunted, and my experience with Pie was limited to a few hunts at widely separated intervals, because in 1975, I moved away. And later that same year, Ben died. Pie was never given much of a chance to prove herself.

It was also about that time that the alterations of the landscape that spelled doom for quail accelerated—changes in forestry and farming practices, whereby hedgerows gave way to pristine edges (deserts for wildlife) and pesticides and herbicides were widely applied, eradicating weeds and bugs (quail food). The farms were lovely to look at, unless you were a quail. More affluent lifestyles transformed those farms into expensive real estate. Waterfront property was especially desirable. Large, new homes with neat, expansive lawns sprung up along the creek shores. New cars needed garages and paved drives. On our farm alone, where once there had been a dozen coveys and three old home places, there were soon two coveys and a dozen homes, built not by "come-hithers," but by Halls and Hursts, family. Our place simply mirrored the rural world around it.

Sweetie Pie II as an adult.

Somehow deer and turkeys adapted to the changes, but quail did not. By any measure—quail sightings, quail hunters, quail harvest—the bobwhite population has fallen about 90 percent in the last thirty years, and appears to still be in decline—the unintended consequences, "collateral damage" if you will, of our new lifestyle, but a quail eradication program could not have done a better job.

So what was I supposed to do in 1996 when my younger son Evan asked me to take him quail hunting? Well, what I did was swallow my pride and take him to a hunting preserve. And I tried not to ruin it for him by constantly reminding him that this is not "real" quail hunting, or how great it was in the "good old days." He'd heard most of that anyway, and understood more or less, but he was born in 1982, and anything before that date is basically prehistory. The other factor favoring a preserve was my sister's Brittany spaniel Sandy. So far, his experience had been limited to field trials and frustrating trips around the farm; she wanted to show him birds. That was relatively easy to arrange. We simply phoned in our

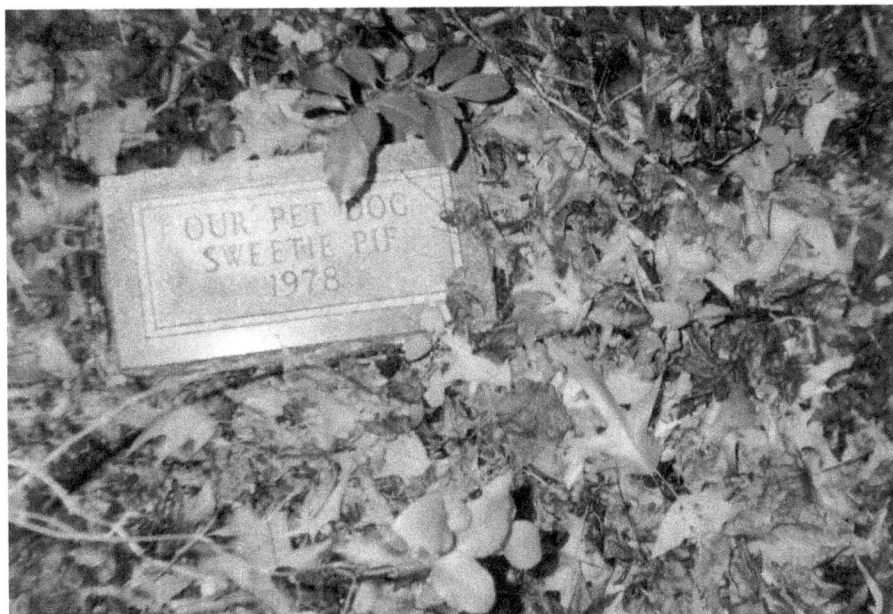

Headstone for Sweetie Pie I. *Ida Hall photo.*

Headstone for Sweetie Pie II. *Ida Hall photo.*

reservation and ordered a certain number of quail and two pheasants to be released prior to our arrival, more like a visit to a restaurant than a hunting trip.

The preserve was a pine plantation near West Point, Virginia, not far from the Mattaponi Indian Reservation; comparisons were hard to avoid—the domestication of birds, trees and people. The terrain consisted of rows of trees interspersed with patches of sorghum and sedge grass; logging roads made for easy walking. We tried to ignore the inconspicuous red flags that marked the vicinity of the released birds, and we reminded ourselves that there were probably holdovers from prior hunters or even wild birds on the property. This pretense made me feel better and may have helped my sister, but Evan and Sandy seemed indifferent to the whole notion of wildness. The dog was euphoric. Evidently pen-raised birds smelled just fine, and they did not fly badly either, not like wild birds—they were quieter—but like quail, nonetheless, and you had better be quick or they would put a pine between you and them before you got a shot off.

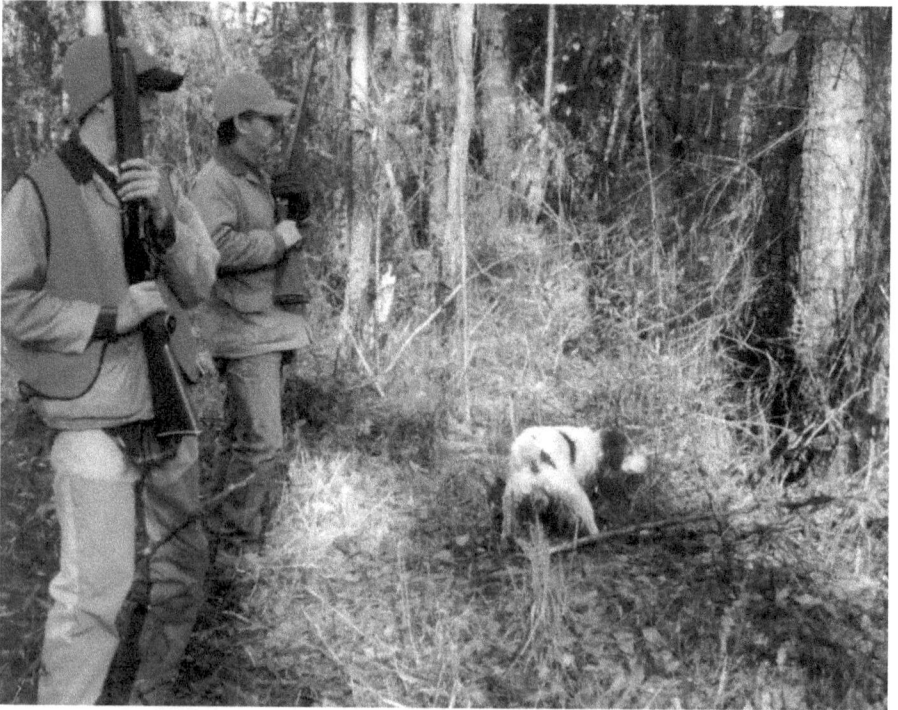

Left to right: Evan Hall, his father (author) and Sandy on a hunting preserve, 1996.

Left to right: Sandy, Ida Hall and Steve Proctor. Same preserve, different day.

Evan was surprisingly quick and, even more surprisingly, quite accurate. I thought back to my repeated failures in the early days of my quail hunting and reminded myself that I was much younger than he, and that those birds were wild, but even making those allowances, I was still amazed at his prowess. He did not grow up hunting, and, except for a brief session with clay targets the day before, he'd hardly ever fired a shotgun, but he was deadly. Finally, I asked him, "What is going on with you? You make this look easy."

He shrugged. "It's a lot like Duck Hunting," he said.

"But you've never even been duck hunting."

"Not real duck hunting. The video game. Duck Hunting the video game."

"Oh God."

Wiseacre that he is, he could not resist rubbing it in. "I always told you video games taught life skills, Dad."

And there you have it, another "Welcome to the Modern World Moment."

Anyhow, we had a few laughs—the dog had more than a few; it was probably the happiest day of his life—and we had quail and pheasant to eat, a nice family outing and photos galore. We even went back once, but only once. My son is not a hunter; neither is his brother Preston nor their cousin Brandon, and there is a sad symmetry in that: the people who miss wild quail and miss hunting them are disappearing just as the quail are disappearing. As wild quail are being replaced by hunting preserves, sporting clays and even video games, quail hunters are being supplanted by their non-hunting offspring. Many people, maybe a majority, see this as "progress"—replacing the barbaric habit of killing wildlife for sport with "non-consumptive" uses of the outdoors, such as biking, hiking or taking long, leisurely walks beside cleanly manicured fields with neat white fences. That's all well and good, but without the evening song serenade of "bobwhite," what would be the point?

CATCH-AND-RELEASE
GILL NETTING

In our family, there was no apparent distinction between commercial and sport fishing. There was much pleasure to be had in commercial fishing, and hook and line–caught fish could also be sold. Therefore, it saddens me to see how in recent years commercial fishermen have received such criticism from sport fishermen. Of all forms of commercial fishing, gill netting gets the worst abuse. Meanwhile, the sporting aspects of gill netting, the skill involved and the aesthetics have been badly neglected.

First of all, where to set the net takes the same sort of knowledge of sea bottom, tides, currents and feeding habits of fish as is required by flats fishing or, for that matter, fishing rivers and ponds. Furthermore, running one hundred fathoms of monofilament net over the stern of a splintery, wooden skiff takes at least as much skill as spin-fishing or fly-casting. The best system I found was to run the net over the ankle of a rubber boot, but one wrong move could snag your toe and send you overboard.

Then comes the tricky business of fishing the net. Whether you are overhauling—boating the fish but not the net—or pulling the entire net into the boat, considerable strength is required, especially in a breeze, because you are dragging the skiff upwind. (Motorized winders and reels, used by the big rigs, eliminate the sporting aspects, just as trolling heavy saltwater tackle behind a forty-foot cruiser removes the sport from hook-and-line fishing: in each instance, the boat is doing the fishing.)

Removing fish from a gill net can be easy or hard depending on your catch. Soft fish, such as spot and menhaden, can be shaken out, but croaker and rock take patience or else you will slice fingers and cut the net. And croaker and rock take two hands, which means that the net must be secured against the gunnel with a knee while the waves toss the boat, and your feet slide on a slurry of fish slime and sea nettle juice. When a large fish flops about in that mess, your eyes are in danger.

And then there are the crabs. Hard-shelled crabs feed on gilled fish, dead or alive. They begin at the tail and advance toward the head. An untended net can yield a catch of fish heads and skeletons, like fish in Halloween costumes or strung up like cut-out paper dolls. A mutilated fish is not fit for sale. Eventually, the greedy crabs become tangled in the net. Thin but tough strands of monofilament catch spines of shell and lodge in the joints of their many legs. Crabs are irascible by nature— hence the term "crabby"—and a tangled crab literally foams at the mouth, like a rabid dog, ready to snap at anything, even a helping hand. It is said that the pincer of a large Jimmy crab can break a finger. The only safe, expeditious solution is to crush the crab with the heel of your boot and shake the remains overboard, where they will be devoured by fish or other crabs.

On the other hand, the pleasures of gill netting can be considerable. The suspense, the telltale throb of line and the first glimpse of fish provide thrills similar to those of hook-and-line fishing. The prettiest gilling comes in the fall, when the water is clear and cool and the sea nettles have gone. The fish do not soften and spoil so fast in the cool fall water, so you don't have to overhaul your net in the middle of the night. A netful of fall spot on a sunny morning glows in the water like a gold necklace.

By far the most sporting form of gill netting is "thrash netting," in which an entire cove or other promising section of shoreline is cordoned off with net. Ideally, each end of net is onshore or in such shallow water that the fish cannot get around. In any case, the fish's natural instinct, when frightened, is to dash for deeper water—where the gill net lies in wait like a fence of nearly invisible mesh. Small lead weights keep the lower line flush against the bottom, while a series of encircling corks floats the top line. In shallow-water fishing, the top-line corks are usually visible as a long arc, not unlike a series of bobbers. Once the set is made, the area enclosed is thrashed: the surface of the water is pounded, traditionally with a long flexible limb, a "thrash pole," but almost any form of noise will do—prop wash, an oar banged against the bottom of the boat, anything to frighten the fish and drive them toward the deep and the net. When the panicky fish hit the net, the corks bob and dance,

The author in the 1990s. This was not catch-and-release gill netting. *Ida Hall photo*.

sink and resurface, just as in bait fishing a bobber signals a bite. It can be quite exciting. You can even release your catch alive and unharmed. It is not common practice, but it can be done.

One hot August day in the late 1960s, when striped bass were still plentiful, I decided to take advantage of an extremely high tide and cast a few soft crabs on the grassy flats behind Hal's house. My skiff stayed at my uncle's dock, because, well, it was his boat, but I had claimed it for the summer. I had removed the middle seat and all else except a single oar, dip net, gas tank, one life jacket and a rusted knife stuck into the stern seat. Except for my spinning rod, it resembled a small but serious work boat, which it was. It smelled like one, too. In the bow, a mound of gill net moldered under a canvas tarp, emitting a perfume of fish, crab and seaweed—Eau de Chesapeake.

I cranked the outboard and eased the skiff into the creek toward Hal's crab floats. In those days, Hal was still fishing traps. The finfish and hard crabs he sold the day he caught them, but the peeler crabs—those about to shed into more valuable soft crabs—he kept in a string of floats between his house and Uncle Ben's. A significant number of crabs do not survive the arduous process of shedding, and Hal let me have the dead soft crabs and peelers to use as bait. The problem was that the death of a soft crab can be difficult to determine. Recently shed soft crabs do not move much. They're exhausted and they have no skeleton, inside or out. They lie around waiting for their shell, their exoskeleton, to harden. Some don't make it. It is very difficult to tell dead from alive, and with bursters—crabs half in and half out of their hard shells—it is almost impossible. Sometimes you just have to make the decision yourself. The tide was already falling and I did not have all day. I scooped up a couple of moribund bursters, declared them dead and scooted around the point to the shallow cove of eelgrass and oyster bed before Hal spotted me.

I cut the engine and let the boat drift in the light breeze. The cove heaved and sighed from a slight groundswell. I baited a single unweighted hook with a hunk of crab and slung it toward the shallows, where it slowly sank. Before it hit bottom, the bait and my line began slicing diagonally away. I tried to set the hook, felt a brief, intriguing resistance and then nothing. The fish was gone. I reeled in; no bait. I added a smaller piece of crab, slightly exposed the point of the hook and heaved it out again, and once again something snatched up the bait and angled away, but once again when I set the hook, there was no fish. It happened again and again.

The fish would pick up the bait and swim with it, but not swallow or even solidly bite it. It was frustrating, and my crab supplies were not unlimited. One of my "dead" bursters was showing signs of life, adding to my burden of guilt.

I sat on the gunnel in the hot sun trying to decide what to do. I wanted to see those fish. I do not mind losing a fish once I've had a good look at it, except for those times when the one look makes losing the fish much worse. Still, all in all, I'd rather know the truth: what was taking my bait? What species? What size? Half the thrill of fishing is solving a mystery. This cove opened into the Bay, which opened into the Atlantic. Theoretically, anything could have been taking my bait. I wanted an answer, and this time I knew how to get it.

I put my spinning rod away and surveyed the dimensions of the problem, that is, the size of the cove, vis a vis the length of my gill net. I could not enclose the entire cove, but I could come pretty close, and I did. In no time, I had net running out over the stern, the sinkers making the lovely hollow sound of lead on wood. I hadn't worn rubber boots because I hadn't planned on setting my net.

It was a good set: both anchors were practically onshore, connected by a smooth, lovely arc of corks. Beauty in fishing is often a matter of perspective. Once, my sister Ida's friend Collin, a fish spotter for the menhaden fleet, showed us aerial photographs of striker boats encircling a huge school of fish. The Bay looked as blue and luminous as the Caribbean, and the dark mass of fish and delicate arc of net were remarkably beautiful—and who ever considered the aesthetic pleasures of the menhaden industry? Well, Collin had; it's why he showed us the pictures. He suspected that my sister and I were likely to appreciate yet another form of fish beauty, and he was right.

The skiff was inside the enclosure when I cranked the engine and began to spin tight circles while pounding the boat bottom with an oar, making quite a racket. I kept my eyes on the corks, which rose and fell from the wake of the boat, but those nearest the channel darted and dipped when the fleeing fish struck the net at full speed. Then the corks quivered as the gilled fish shimmied and wriggled. I motored to one end of the net, cut the engine and began fishing the net as quickly as possible, before the fish suffocated. It wasn't long before I raised the first fish, a rock about eighteen inches long, still frisky and alive. Working fast, I plied he monofilament from his gill plates and released the fish on the Bay side of the net so I would not catch him twice.

All told, I caught and released about two dozen rock, all virtually identical in size and none seriously injured. I had solved the puzzle and had not hurt the fish. All in all, it was a very satisfying experience. I sat on the gunnel to enjoy the moment. I had fooled those fish; so what if I used a net? Fishing is fishing. They frustrated me; I paid them back and then let them go. I had used the tools at my disposal; sometimes that might mean a secret lure; this time it meant a net. Another triumph of human resourcefulness, or so I believed at the time.

The trouble was that Hal had witnessed the entire scene from his bedroom window. My commotion had awakened him from his afternoon nap. Groggy from sleep and from the heavy, wet summer heat, he was not sure exactly what he had seen. When I motored back into the creek, he was standing at the end of his dock smoking a Salem. He waved me over. My first thought was that he wanted to know how many crabs I'd taken, but that was not it at all. Always curious about fish, he wanted to know what I'd caught.

As I eased into his dock, he grabbed the gunnel and craned his neck to see my catch, but there was nothing to see except one dead, or nearly dead, soft crab. His leathery, lined face was a picture of confusion. "Where're the fish?" he asked. "I saw you picking some out."

"Oh, I caught a couple of dozen school-sized rock," I said. Like an idiot, I was still feeling proud of my accomplishment. "But I put them all back."

"What'd you do that for?"

"I didn't really need 'em," I said. "I just wanted to see what was taking my bait." It was slowly sinking in that I wasn't exactly a hero or clever guy in Hal's eyes, and at the moment his were the only ones that counted.

He shook his head in disgust. "Just throwing money overboard," he said, his voice trailing off. He could not believe that anyone, much less a member of his family, would throw away fish that sold for forty-five cents a pound. I might as well have tossed a ten-dollar bill out the car window. He gave me a withering look that said I never had been and never would be a real commercial fishermen; then he flicked his cigarette into the water and walked disgustedly back to the house.

So it turned out that there was a distinction in our family between commercial fishing and sport fishing after all. I just had not realized it until that moment when I saw it in Hal's eyes and heard it in his voice. Commercial fishing could be fun, but it wasn't meant to be a game. It was not pitch and catch; it wasn't baseball. It was serious business, life or death for fish and a livelihood for the fisherman. And maybe city people ought not to play at it if they did not comprehend those simple facts.

Hal was right, of course. I did not have what it took to be a real commercial fisherman, never had and never would. After a while, I stopped wanting it, but that came years later.

HUNTING VERSUS POACHING

When your family's waterfowling traditions extend back to the days of market hunting, it is hard to think of shooting ducks over a few grains of corn as a crime. You understand that it is against the law; you just do not feel that it is wrong. Some in our family sincerely believed that a corn-fed duck was a healthier duck and, therefore, more likely to survive the long winter and the rigors of migration. We all believed that they tasted better.

There was never much discussion on the subject of why or whether to bait ducks. It was axiomatic that you shot ducks over bait or you did not shoot ducks. If you did not bait, the ducks would find someone who did. If they found no bait on Dividing Creek, the ducks would move to Indian Creek or Dameron Marsh. One way or another, the ducks would find corn; the only question was whose. So, we reasoned, why not ours?

In the market-hunting days, the supply of ducks must have seemed inexhaustible, and even in my time, diving ducks were so plentiful that when a flock lifted off out in the Bay, it resembled a plume of smoke from a passing freighter en route to Baltimore. Ducks were no different from crabs, oysters and fish—a crop to be harvested, part of the Bay's never-ending bounty. Not to harvest them would have been wasteful. "God gave man dominion over all animals," Hal was fond of quoting, and the Bible carried far more weight with Hal than did game laws crafted by flawed and fallible men.

There was a science to baiting ducks. You could not just throw corn out willy-nilly and expect to succeed. That method might attract ducks but would likely draw game wardens as well. Ideally, you would bait a

Left to right: Steve Dulany Proctor and Snowden Hall III (IV). Widgeon and geese, probably from Mud Creek, 1959.

day or so before you planned to hunt so that by the day of the hunt, the incriminating evidence, every grain of corn, would be gone. And you re-baited after the hunt. Of course, things did not always work out according to plans; sometimes a person, even Hal, could get careless, overconfident, because even the best of men were flawed and fallible. "Only one perfect Man ever lived," Hal said, and he was not referring to himself, or even to his friend, cousin and hunting companion, Buster Conway, a waterman of such notable integrity that my father invariably referred to him as the "Salt of the Earth." I never heard my father mention Buster's name without adding that phrase, as if "Salt of the Earth" was part of his name or title, "Buster Conway, SOE." Perhaps it was Buster's unimpeachable morality, and Hal's luck, that protected them from the game wardens one cold, gray morning on the Sand Point.

The Sand Point, long since gone, was a hook of land on the north end of Bluff Point that created a cove on Jarvis Creek, a perfect place for a duck blind. With a northeast wind, the ducks would pitch straight into the blind. That morning, Hal and Buster had already killed and retrieved several scaup, which they had left in the skiff along with a bucket of corn. The ducks were in plain view, the corn was in the bow covered with a burlap bag and the skiff was tucked under tall grass. When the wardens appeared, Hal and Buster were back in the blind awaiting the next flight of ducks; a few flakes of snow pinged against their oilskin jackets. Rather abruptly, a boat swung around the Sand Point and came ashore immediately in front of the blind. Hal's and Buster's comments at that moment have been lost to posterity, but one thing we can know for sure: Buster did not curse or take the Lord's name in vain. Always the gentlemen, the hunters left the blind and came to greet the two young wardens.

The four men stood on the wet sand, shivering and making small talk, the wardens trying to act as if they just happened to be in the neighborhood, as if this was a social visit, and—by the way—they might as well take a look at the hunters' licenses and duck stamps and make sure that their auto-loaders were properly plugged. Then the wardens kicked around in the grass to make sure no one had hidden an illegal duck and finally, almost apologetically, they needed to check the boat registration and to check the ducks that Hal and Buster had already "confessed" to killing. Those were legal ducks, more or less—definitely within the limit—but the way that wardens acted, any hunting seemed like a crime.

As Hal and Buster followed the wardens to the skiff and that poorly concealed bucket of corn, they must have felt like condemned men walking to their execution. First, the wardens checked the necks of the three scaup, carefully palpating the craws for even a single kernel of incriminating evidence. "They're clean."

"'Course they're clean," Buster said, feeling and sounding more indignant by the minute. The very idea of these two young pups treating Hal and him like criminals! He and Hal had been fishing, oystering and hunting those waters longer than these wardens had been alive.

When the heavyset warden leaned over to examine the boat registration that was nailed up under the bow, his supporting hand came to rest on the burlap bag covering the bucket of corn. If Hal or Buster had had a heart condition, now's the time it would have manifested itself. But, as it happened, the warden was so absorbed in checking the validity of the registration that he never bothered to look under that bag. He never discovered the corn that was within inches of his fingers! Instead, his inspection complete, he straightened up, stretched his back and, sounding almost disappointed, said, "Well, it looks like you boys are awright this morning."

At which point Buster rose to his full height of well over six feet and, his voice brimming with righteous indignation, said, "And you will find us right each and every time you check us too."

"Good, that's how we like to find people," the warden said, unconvincingly, and off they went.

That was the end of it—almost. But it has never really ended—and let's hope it doesn't—because over the years Buster's words—"And you will find us right each and every time you check us too"—have been engraved in our family's oral tradition and repeated whenever and wherever the occasion calls—weddings, funerals or family reunions. The story has become a parable, but the lesson, as I understand it, is not how to break the law and get away with it. The lesson is that moral rectitude will always be rewarded. The real crime would have been for those wardens to find that corn and besmirch the good name of Buster Conway, Salt of the Earth.

Punt-gunning was another popular way of harvesting ducks in the old days. The punt was a shallow skiff, pointed on both ends; the gun was an enormous single-barrel shotgun, mounted on the bow like a cannon. The hunter used hand paddles to sneak into range of a flock of ducks, usually after dark, and would then cut loose with a single great blast that often killed fifty or more ducks at once. It sounds barbaric, and maybe it is, but it is still legal in daylight hours in—of all unlikely places—England. In many states in this country, shooting deer over bait and salt licks is perfectly legal. In

Buster Conway, "Salt of the Earth." *Arthur Conway photo.*

Maine, though baiting deer and ducks is illegal, most black bears are killed over bait—legally. Clearly, when it comes to hunting methods, we are not dealing in moral absolutes.

My closest brush with anything resembling punt-gunning came when my famously upright father and his brother Ben made a nighttime sneak on a flock of geese feeding in Oyster Creek. Hardly your typical criminal profile: Ben was an elementary school principal; my father Snowden was a prominent physician who never lied, cheated or shot over the limit, but he sometimes baited ducks and on this occasion hunted after dark, and I suppose technically you would have to say that he "contributed to the delinquency of a minor." That would have been me, a boy of about ten, who insisted on being taken along on this great adventure. The illicit preparations alone were exciting enough: these two role models rigging a skiff for a night hunt.

Ben wrapped the oarlocks in burlap to silence them and mounted a car headlight on the bow, which he connected with cables to a twelve-volt battery beside the middle seat, where he would sit and row. My father sat in the bow, not with a cannon, but with the next best thing, his L.C. Smith twelve-gauge side-by-side, bored full and modified, a perfect waterfowling piece. I sat in the stern and kept quiet—for me, a talker, perhaps the hardest job of all.

In those days, about fifty-five years ago, Mud and Oyster Creeks were sizable bodies of water, about sixty acres in all. Mud Creek was especially rich in aquatic vegetation, and in the spring one particular cove near the barn would be crowded with migrating puddle ducks. Many an Easter I would creep through the brush and honeysuckle beside Mud Creek admiring the beautiful widgeon, teal and mallard from a proximity—twenty yards or fewer—that would have been impossible in the fall or winter. The ducks seemed to understand that this time of year they were safe and would not be hunted. To shoot a duck in the spring, when their minds were on migrating and mating, would not only have been illegal; it would have been wrong. That really would have been poaching and would have been condemned by everyone in our family, hunter and non-hunter alike, because it would have violated the laws of man and nature. It was even in the Bible, "To everything there is a season," meaning, as I understood it, a real season, as opposed to the arbitrary and capricious dates set by man.

But now it was winter, and geese were fair game, except that this flock was making legal hunting exceedingly difficult: they rafted up in the Bay during the daylight hours, usually flew into Oyster Creek after dark and flew out before daybreak. It was as if the geese were taunting us. They were taking advantage of the regulations and practically demanding to be hunted at night.

In retrospect, I believe it was the teamwork between my father and uncle that makes this moment glow so warmly in my memory. Ben and his brother were very different men. My father Snowden was ambitious and professionally driven; Ben was happiest puttering around the farm, repairing a piece of equipment, planting a garden, curing hams or building a boat. My father moved away; Ben stayed home. Ben was a warm, affectionate man; my father was aloof even among his immediate family.

Snowden liked to bird hunt; Ben did not hunt until late in his life and then only to accommodate his dog. Ben was "handy": he built his own house and several boats and could fix anything. If my father needed something fixed, he hired it out. But on this project, they could combine Ben's love of tinkering with my father's love of hunting; on this occasion, the two brothers worked as one.

It was a moonless night with no wind. We waited until well after dark before easing the skiff out into Mud Creek, Ben at the oars, my father in the bow. They spoke in whispers; I spoke not at all, and there was no need to speak. As the skiff moved silently into the run connecting the two creeks, the stand of pines to the west loomed like a black wall to the west, while to the east the spooky silhouettes of twisted pines, persimmon and pin oak haunted the beach. As we entered Oyster Creek, the soft cackling of the feeding geese was faintly audible an uncertain distance ahead.

Barely visible in the starlight, a rim of trees formed a low horizon at the far end of Oyster Creek, but below the trees was absolute blackness. It was impossible to visually judge distances in the dark. Ben rowed on instinct, memory and by the sound of the geese. Initially, even to a child's ear, the cackling sounded as calm and relaxed as dinner table conversation. Then, as the skiff drew closer, the tone changed from idle chat to querulous voices of concern, higher pitched and louder. Ben and my father exchanged urgent whispers. "What do you think?" "What do you think?"

We were close, but how close was impossible to know, until at last Ben clamped the cable to that final battery terminal. Then came an explosion of light and sound, a roar of noise—chaos in the air. The shotgun blasts were barely louder than the honks, cries, squawks of the startled geese, which were already disappearing over the Bay as echoes of gunfire rumbled back and forth across the creek. Then it was quieter than ever. Ben angled the light across the water, searching, and then out over the beach. There was not a single downed goose to be seen. "Damn!" my father said, in a rare outburst of profanity, but this was a night of no rules, of renegade behavior, relatively speaking. "I don't think I touched a feather."

"I might have turned that light on just a few seconds too soon," Ben said.

"You didn't have much choice. They were about to spook."

"Well, one thing's for sure. We put a pretty good scare in that bunch."

"We did that."

Then we all laughed. Who cared if we got skunked?

Snowden C. Hall Jr. (III) in a skiff rigged for navigating the shallow ditch and even shallower Mud Creek, 1960s. In the background is the Sand Point (aka Jarvis Point).

Ben rowed us back with the headlight off; no need to attract any more attention than necessary. Riding back, there was no second guessing, no finger pointing and no recriminations. They never tried it again, either. Time was a factor—my father was a busy doctor—but I doubt it was the only factor. I think overall that, goose or no goose, they considered the expedition a success. No point trying to duplicate it.

One thing that strikes about this incident in retrospect is this: my father was very sensitive to public opinion, very aware of his position as prominent physician in the town of Danville. Later, he would serve on the State Board of Medical Examiners. He never liked anyone in the family doing anything to embarrass him or compromise his reputation in the community, but if he ever worried about being arrested for hunting after dark or baiting ducks, I never heard him mention it. Not once. From my perspective, hunting, legal or not, always brought out the best in him. It made him seem more human, and never more so than on that night in Oyster Creek. I am particularly grateful that I was allowed to go along on that occasion and witness illegal hunting—I would never call it "poaching"—as an act of brotherly love. And no geese were harmed in the creation of this memory.

CLOSE TO NATURE

Why would a grown woman want to go out gill netting? That's what Lester couldn't understand. It wasn't the same as when he'd had the big boat and Evelyn was a little girl and would sit up on the cabin, safely out of harm's way. The big boat was gone; he'd told her that. Now she'd get her clothes dirty; now she'd smell like fish. "That's the whole idea," she said. She wanted to get her clothes dirty. She wanted to smell like fish. Why would a grown woman want to smell like fish? That's what Lester couldn't understand.

Lester was standing on the end of his dock smoking a cigarette. In the early morning light, he couldn't see the other houses lining the cove. It was as if the whole place was his again. Then a light came on across the creek. Evelyn was up.

He flicked his cigarette into the water and loaded two bushel baskets and an extra tank of gas into his skiff. He had no idea where she'd sit. He'd removed the middle seat to make room for fishing gear. She'd need a fairly substantial place to sit. As he remembered, she was pretty wide in the hips. C.E. Lee once said, "Evelyn Harmon Hoyt is so broad abeam she ought to paint her name across her stern." C.E. Lee was often saying such things about women, usually his ex-wives, and Evelyn wasn't anywhere near as large as C.E. said, but she would need a sturdy seat. Lester doubted that an upturned bushel basket would do the job. He found a fish box that was rugged and fairly clean and set it upside down near the bow.

Then the light went off across the creek; a door slammed; a car engine started, revved, its sound sank into the distance and then was loud again in Lester's lane, then silent. Soon Evelyn came strolling down onto Lester's dock. "Don't you just love this time of day?" she asked. "It's so quiet and peaceful."

"Should have been here a few minutes ago. It was really peaceful then," Lester said.

"Same old Lester," Evelyn said. She was wearing jeans and a T-shirt. She had cut her hair, but it was as black as ever. And she'd put on weight, but still wasn't fat, just stocky. C.E. Lee once said that Evelyn was built more like a quarter horse than a thoroughbred, and as a matter of fact, all her marriages had been sprints.

Evelyn took a deep breath and let it out very slowly. "This salt air is so wonderful. You can't get air like this in the city."

"You can take some back with you if you want," Lester said.

Evelyn climbed down into the skiff and stuffed a canvas bag under the bow. "I brought some beach things," she said. "I thought, if you didn't mind, you could drop me off on the Sand Point on the way back in. If it's not too much trouble."

"No indeed," Lester said. "I can drop you on the way out, if you want."

"You haven't changed a bit."

Evelyn sat on her fish box, and Lester pulled the starter rope. The engine fired on the first pull. He backed the skiff away from the dock through a cloud of fumes.

At the first channel marker, Evelyn pointed to a pair of nesting ospreys and looked back at Lester to make sure he had seen them too. She gestured just as enthusiastically to a flock of seagulls perched on the Sand Point, as if they too were objects of great natural beauty, instead of, in Lester's opinion, seafaring pigeons. When the sun burned through the mist like a flame blazing through a pile of dried brush, Evelyn looked like she would burst.

Lester cut the engine at the downwind clump of Clorox bottles he used as a buoy and worked some slack into the net. "You're lucky, you know that?" Evelyn said.

"How's that?" Lester asked.

"To be able to work out here in such beautiful surroundings, so close to nature. Sometimes I feel like the city is destroying me."

"It's not always like this," Lester said as he was struggling to raise the heavy lead line. He didn't elaborate, but sometimes the Bay was cruel and rough and cold. If you romanticized the Bay, she'd kill you. She killed Otha, threw him overboard and drowned him. So don't tell Lester how lucky he was to work so close to nature. Tell Otha. You couldn't get any closer to nature than Otha was. He was part of it.

Lester pulled slowly, steadily down the net. A few spot appeared at irregular intervals, murky white forms near the lead line. They sort of resembled a strand of pearls, not store-bought cultured pearls, but real ones, with funny, irregular shapes that he sometimes found in his oysters. Lester wasn't denying that there was great beauty in nature, but in his opinion, nature was most beautiful when she was made to do man's bidding. Lester had a working relationship with nature, and no question who was boss.

The prettiest gilling came with the cool weather in the fall when the water was clear and there were no sea nettles. This was not pretty gilling. This was midsummer gilling, with hot, murky water, fish spoiling in the net, too many menhaden and crabs and, worst of all, the sea nettles that clotted the net in gelatinous globs, making it heavy for Lester to lift and easy for the fish to see. Underwater, a clean net was all but invisible; a net full of sea nettles was like a wall of Jell-O.

Evelyn was soon restless and wanted something to do. Lester let her pull the top line, the corks. Most of the fish, being bottom feeders, gilled near the leads, which Lester was pulling. "That's not fair," she said. "You're getting all the fish."

"That's how it is some days," Lester said. "Some days they gill high, and some days they gill low."

She seemed to believe him. Lester was amazed. Then a fish showed up on her side of the net. It was a croaker, also called "hardhead" because of its hard, sharp gill plates. "You better let me do that one," Lester said. "They can be right mean to get out."

"You just take care of your end of the net. I'll take care of mine." Evelyn struggled to free a strand of net that was embedded in a gill plate. When she tried to force it, the gill plate sliced her thumb. "Ow," she said. She shoved her thumb into her mouth.

"I told you those things were mean," Lester said. But when he reached over to take the fish, she pushed his hand away.

"I hope you don't think I'm giving up that easily," she said.

He let her have the fish. He didn't want to fight with her. She had a fierce, determined look on her face, as if that fish meant a lot to her. Lester looked up at the sun. It had shrunk to the size of a dime and glowed like molten silver. He wiped his forehead and looked off into the distance for the other buoy, then at his watch. At the rate they were going, the fish already in the boat would spoil before they reached the other end. He looked back at Evelyn. She was still struggling with the same mesh.

"Just break the darn bar," Lester said.

"What?"

"Just break that one mesh that's holding it."

"Oh, why didn't you say that sooner?"

"I don't like to break any more than I have to."

Evelyn tried to break the strand of net but couldn't get her fingers under it well enough to apply pressure.

"That monofilament is right rugged stuff," Lester said. "Not like those old cotton nets."

"It's not that tough," Evelyn said. "I just can't get a grip on it."

When she tried to reposition the fish, it drove the spines of its dorsal fin into the heel of her hand. "Damn it!" She dropped the fish and placed her hand back into her mouth.

Lester reached over and snapped the strand of net as if it had been sewing thread. The fish flopped around on the bottom of the boat. Evelyn kicked it toward the stern. "Be careful," Lester said. "Those spines will go right through a tennis shoe."

While Evelyn licked her wounds, Lester pulled down the net as quickly as possible. He wasn't glad that she got hurt, but if she did have to get herself hurt, he was grateful for the location of the wound. With her hand in her mouth, she couldn't talk or help. But Evelyn wasn't that easily defeated. Soon she was bored and restless again.

"There must be something I can do," she said.

"Not really," Lester said. "Gill netting is pretty much a one-man operation. I told you that."

"I can at least bail the boat out," she said. Several inches of sea water and fish slime had accumulated in the bottom of the boat. "Haven't you got a scoop?"

He tossed her the cut-up plastic milk carton he used as a scoop. He was about to warn her to be careful of the sea nettle juice that mixed with the sea water when he felt a heavy throbbing far down in the water and forgot about Evelyn.

When small fish such as spot gilled, the net usually closed their gills and killed them. But a fish too large to gill would tangle a corner of its mouth in one mesh, stay alive and be only lightly held by the net. What Lester felt was large and very much alive. He knelt down and peered into the water to see which side of the net the fish had hit. He raised the net very gently until the pale outline of a large gray trout came into view. Lester formed a sort of hammock around the fish and eased the trout—six or seven pounds—into the skiff. When he flipped the net over, the fish fell out of its own weight and began thrashing wildly about in the bottom of the boat toward Evelyn.

"I'll get him for you," Evelyn said. She reached for the fish, and the swish of its tail sent a shower of sea water and slime into Evelyn's face. "Jesus!" she said covering her eyes with her hands.

Lester came forward, shoved his fingers into the trout's gills and slung the fish into a bushel basket. "Put some water in your eyes. That's the only thing that'll take the fire out. Bay water."

"Don't worry about me, okay? I can take care of myself."

Lester returned to the stern and began pulling along the net. "Those darn sea nettles are the dickens anyway," Lester said. "Otha used to say that one day a man would find a use for sea nettles, and then we'd all..."

"Lester!"

He was quiet for a while. If she didn't want to know what Otha said about sea nettles, then to heck with her. He wasn't glad she'd gotten sea nettle juice in her eyes. He wouldn't wish that on anyone. But maybe now she'd look at things a little differently. Maybe sea nettle juice in her eyes would improve her vision.

When Evelyn's eyes stopped watering, she sat on her fish box and watched, but Lester could tell that she was getting restless again. After a while, she reached up and took the top line. "I can at least do this much," she said.

He didn't argue. He was tired of trying to save her from herself. Soon a huge tangle of net came onboard. In the center of the gnarl was a hard crab eating a dead fish. The tail had been cleaned to the bone. "It's an amazing thing to me," Lester said. "His predicament hasn't even fazed his appetite. I've seen it many a time, and it never ceases to amaze me."

"What are you talking about?"

"There's no way he's getting out of that mess alive. Yet he just keeps right on eating. I guess there's a lesson in that, but darned if I know what it is."

"What do you mean he won't get out alive?" Evelyn asked, pulling the net her way.

"You won't get him out in one piece." Monofilament had a way of hanging in the crevasses of the crab's legs and on the sharp edges of its shell.

"That's what you think," she said. "This is one thing I'm good at: messes!"

Evelyn evidently had taken Lester's statement as a challenge, though he had not meant it as one, and she had plunged into her work with grim determination. Lester sighed, sat down on the gunnel and lit a cigarette. "Even if you can get him out, it'll take too long. You spend ten minutes on every crab, and all your fish'll spoil before you get in."

"You just hold your horses."

Lester looked off into the Bay. A couple of crab potters, a few sport fishermen and not a fish trap to be seen. A sad sight. He never thought he'd see the day.

Evelyn was down to the last layer of net holding the big male crab. Its pincers were clamped tightly shut on the dead fish. The crab's eyes pivoted on little turrets; foam oozed from its mouth.

"You be careful," Lester said. "A Jimmy crab that size can break a finger."

"Thanks, that's just the sort of encouragement I need." She struggled with a strand of net caught in a leg joint. Her hands were shaking slightly. Lester wiped his forehead and looked at his watch. "Just be patient," Evelyn said. "I won't be long."

The crab released the fish with one claw and snapped at Evelyn. "Stop it, you stupid thing. I'm on your side."

"Let me show you how I do it," Lester said.

"Just hold on. I'm doing all right."

She began talking to the crab in a soothing tone of voice, trying to persuade it that she understood its predicament. She even stroked its shell; the second time she tried, the crab clamped down on her thumb. "Ow!" she yelled and ripped her thumb free, tearing the skin.

Lester pulled the tangle of net his way. "Here's how I do it," he said, centering the crab on the gunnel and placing the heel of his boot on the back of the crab's shell.

"No!" Evelyn said, as the shell shattered with a loud crack.

Lester ground the crab into mush and then dropped the net overboard. Pieces of crab drifted off in a yellow stain as the net slowly unraveled and sank.

Evelyn shook her head back and forth; she was crying. "I almost had it," she said. "I could have worked it out. All I needed was a little more time. Why'd you have to kill it?" She turned and faced the other way. "So cruel."

Lester didn't know what to say. He'd never seen anybody get that upset over a crab before. If he'd known it meant that much to her, he wouldn't have crushed it. He didn't know she'd grown so attached to it or he wouldn't have killed it. "There'll be more crabs," he finally said. "The Bay's full of crabs. Otha used to say winter dredging would ruin the crabbing, but…"

"Please!" Evelyn whispered.

Lester was silent for a while. He knew he shouldn't have brought her. She had been away too long. She'd spent too much time in the city. She was in the restaurant business—she'd probably served more crabs than he'd ever caught—and here she was crying over one crab!

When he was nearly at the end of his net, Lester felt a heavy throb. He hoped for another big gray trout, but it was a dog shark. He pulled the dull gray fish quickly in. Normally, he'd take a dog shark by the tail, slam its head against the side of the boat and watch it swim off upside down, but he handled this one like a baby and released it alive. "I don't think he's any worse for wear," he said.

At the end of the net, Lester let the boat drift in the breeze. He washed his hands overboard, peeled his oilskins down and shook a cigarette from its pack. As he leaned back against the outboard and smoked his cigarette, he looked at his hands, which burned where the salt water had hit the many cuts and scrapes. His hands were a mess. They looked like a pair of worn-out leather gloves. If they hadn't been attached to his wrists, he'd have thrown them out.

Evelyn was still turned the other way when she started talking. "Do you remember when I used to go out fishing with you when I was little?" she asked without turning around.

"Sure I do," Lester said. "You used to go out with me a lot."

"Almost every morning some summers. You were fishing traps then. I used to ask you so many questions I'm surprised you didn't throw me overboard."

"You weren't that much trouble," Lester said. "Not the way I remember it."

"You know, looking back, I think those were the happiest days of my life. That's sad, isn't it?"

"I don't know if it is or not," Lester said. "Those were right good times. I don't know if I've had any better ones myself."

"But that's different!" Evelyn said, turning now and looking straight at Lester. "You're a commercial fisherman. I'm a businesswoman. I'm thirty-eight years old. I've been married. I've been a lot of things. And to look back over my life and realize that the happiest time was when I was ten years old, on a goddamn fishing boat…" She shook her head. "It's tragic. No, no that's too big a word for it. It's pathetic, that's what it is. Pathetic."

She looked like she was going to cry again, and Lester didn't know what to say. So he just cranked the engine. "These fish are going to go soft if I don't get them on some ice soon," he said. Then he threw the engine into gear and headed for the Sand Point. To see where he was going he had to look past Evelyn, who was still staring at him. Soon she turned and looked inshore.

Lester cut the engine in the shallow water. Evelyn tossed her bag up onto the beach and then hopped overboard and held the bow of the skiff off so it wouldn't rub. She seemed to be feeling better. "I'm sorry if I loused up our morning," she said.

"You didn't hurt anything. I'm sorry you didn't have a better time."

"It was fine. I've just lost my touch with fish."

"You can go with me tomorrow if you want to."

"That's nice of you, but I don't guess I will."

"Suit yourself. Are your eyes all right?"

"They're fine. Hands too. Superficial wounds only. Bye Lester." She gave the bow a hard shove and turned and walked up the beach.

Lester pulled the starter rope, and the engine caught immediately. It almost always did. It was an Evinrude. It was the most reliable engine he had ever owned. It started easy and ran smooth at all speeds. As he moved out into the deep water, the engine purred like a cat, like the big tom that slept at the foot of Lester's bed. It was a very soothing sound, like music to his ears. Sometimes he thought it was the only music he would ever understand.

ARROWHEADS

E ven as an adolescent, Roy still liked looking for arrowheads. In the spring, the best places for finding them were the bare fields before they were plowed, but in the summer, it was the bayshore. The best part of the bayshore was its southern tip, Bluff Point, where the beach ended among the marshlands of Barnacle Creek. Here, far from houses, roads, cars and people, Roy would wade for hours in the tidal pools formed by the tussocks of stubble, where the marsh itself was being washed away. The shallow pools acted like miners' pans and collected a sediment of bark, pebbles, broken glass, shells and stones.

You almost never saw the entire arrowhead. You had to look for clues: a corner, a tip, a certain color or texture of stone—scalloped edges of a piece of chert, the corrugated surfaces of milky quartz—that told you it was not bark, not shell, not ordinary stone, but *worked* rock. Only then would you pick it up. Even then you were usually wrong. Black chert turned into bark, crumbled in your hand; white quartz became an oyster shell; the gray, finely grained stone, a certain spearhead, was a barnacle streaked with mud. But every now and then a tip would be exactly that; you'd flip it with your finger and feel the resistance of the rest of the stone sunk in the mud. That instant of recognition, of discovery, never stopped exciting Roy.

The first thing he would do with every find was wash it off. The second was admire the stone. He knew the names, dates, uses of the various styles of arrowheads. He even knew that "arrowhead" was not the correct name. "Projectile point" was what they should be called, but who cared? Analysis

was for later. The bayshore at Barnacle Creek was not a place for science. It was wild and uninhabited, and except for erosion, it probably had not changed in hundreds or thousands of years. It was a place to forget what you had learned from books and to let your imagination run wild. Sometimes Roy would hold an arrowhead in his hand, shut his eyes, see what images played across his mind and wonder what hands had held that stone before his, and what or whom those hands had touched.

Searching the shallow pools almost hypnotized Roy, and he would lose all track of time except that told by the tide and sun. No point looking when the tide reached a certain height or the sun the wrong angle. Then he would sit on the beach for a while and enjoy the solitude. He almost never saw another soul on that section of beach. Even a footprint was a mystery: a crabber in search of washed-up buoys? A trap fisherman after stakes? To see an actual person was a shock. And one day to see a woman in a two-piece bathing suit—at first he thought his eyes had lied to him. He thought his fantasies, which were not always about Indians, had gotten the best of him.

Then, as the woman came closer, he recognized her. It was his cousin, Evelyn Harmon Hoyt. He felt embarrassed because, even though he still liked looking for arrowheads, he thought of it as a childish pursuit, something he probably should have outgrown and just hadn't quite yet. And because Evelyn in the past had always treated him like a child, and he didn't want her to. He stood up, brushed the sand from his bathing suit and sauntered over to let her see how tall he'd gotten.

She took off her dark glasses and squinted at him. "Roy?" she said. "I heard you were down, but I still hardly recognized you. You're all grown up."

He shrugged. This was a little more like it. "What brings you all the way down to this end of the beach?" Roy asked.

"I felt like walking. Felt like being alone. Lester dropped me on the Sand Point. I helped him fish his gill net."

"Oh, yeah? How'd he do?" Roy didn't go out with Lester now that he had sold the big boat.

"All right, I guess. A couple of bushels. He seemed satisfied."

"What were they?"

"I don't remember. Trout, spot, crabs, sea nettles, who knows?" She did not seem to want to talk about fish. She held out her hurt hand. "Look what happened to me," she said. There was a cut on the heel of her hand surrounded by a bruise. "A big Jimmy crab."

"You're not supposed to pick them up by their claws," Roy said.

"Very funny. You sound just like Lester, you know?"

Roy took it as a compliment, though it did not sound like she meant it as one.

"Is my eye still red?" Evelyn said, leaning toward Roy.

"A little," Roy said. Evelyn smelled like suntan lotion and perfume and maybe hairspray. He couldn't separate all the aromas, but they were different from anything he had ever smelled before, more exotic and exciting.

"Sea nettle juice," she said, moving away, rubbing her eye again.

"I know that does hurt," Roy said. "Let me look at that again."

She leaned back toward him and he took a closer look at her eye. Her closeness, the sweet aroma of the lotion and the hot sun had a strange effect on Roy. He felt woozy, in a pleasant way, as if he'd had a beer or two. "Yeah, he got you all right," he said.

She moved back, removed a small makeup kit from her beach bag and checked herself in the mirror, first the eyes and then her hair. A few wet curls were plastered to her forehead by perspiration. "I look like a wreck," she said.

"You look fine," Roy said. He meant it. He liked how she looked. She looked more sophisticated than the girls he knew. Part of it may have been her reputation within the family. Evelyn was mysterious and worldly. Roy didn't know the specifics. He'd always been considered too young to know. So what Roy imagined was probably much worse than what he had not been told. All he knew for sure was that she'd been married more than once and owned a restaurant in Baltimore.

When Evelyn finished tidying up her face and hair, she closed the compact with a sharp snap. "So, anyway," Evelyn said, "what are you doing all the way down here by yourself?"

"Just walking," Roy said, "and looking to see if anything of interest had washed up on the beach since I was here last."

Evelyn smiled. "You too, huh? Find anything?"

"A few arrowheads," he said casually, as if he'd just happened upon them.

"Oh, neat. Can I see them?"

Roy reached into the pocket of his bathing suit and showed her what he'd found: four arrowheads. Two were broken at the tip; another was intact but fairly ordinary, but the fourth was the finest arrowhead Roy had ever found, ever seen. It was formed from two different shades of chert; the base was chestnut brown and the tip was cream. The two shades met in the center of the stone at a sharp angle, the same angle as that formed by the tip of the arrowhead.

Evelyn's fingers went straight to that stone. "It's beautiful," she said. "It's a work of art. I had no idea the Indians did that sort of work."

"Most people don't," Roy said.

Then Evelyn held the arrowhead, tip down, against her chest. "It would make a beautiful pendant." She looked up and batted her eyes at Roy. "I don't suppose you'd consider…"

Roy sighed and shifted his feet. "I'd rather not part with that one," he said, deepening his voice, hoping to sound detached and scientific. "This one is of considerable archaeological interest. I'm sort of a collector."

Evelyn sagged and tucked the stone back into his pocket. "Okay," she said, sounding like a disappointed little girl.

"I'll tell you what," Roy said. "I'll show you where to find one on your own. It would mean more to you if you found your own."

She brightened. "Will you help me look?"

Roy checked his watch and the tide. "I promised Lester I'd help him pull his skiff up when the tide was high enough. It needs to be caulked and recoppered." Evelyn made a sad face. "But I'll help get you started," Roy added. "Okay?"

"I guess," she said without much enthusiasm. She set her beach bag on the sand and followed Roy down to the tussocks and tidal pools. "It's mud!" she said.

"No, it isn't. It's just a different texture of sand."

"It feels like mud."

"It comes right off. It won't hurt you. Come on." He took her hand and led her through the tidal pools. He told her what to look for, the tips and edges, the texture of rock. "You almost never see the whole arrowhead." He told her to try and ignore the shells, sticks, pebbles and other debris, but he had a hard time following his own advice, because every time Evelyn leaned over to examine a piece of bark or shell Roy could see down the front of her bathing suit. He began having mixed feelings about wanting her to find an arrowhead. Soon he heard himself encouraging her to examine what were obviously not arrowheads, just so she would lean over. He was not terribly proud of himself, but he was not ashamed, either. Somehow in this remote place, where there was more evidence of primitive man than of so-called civilization, it seemed okay to let your instincts loose.

But after a while he realized that no matter how far she leaned over, there was only so much he could see. Besides, she was his cousin. Also, the tide was rising, almost flood, and there was Lester to think of. After twenty minutes of looking, Evelyn didn't seem any closer to finding an arrowhead than when she'd begun. Finally, Roy reached into his pocket and found his second-best arrowhead, and when Evelyn wasn't looking, tossed it out in front of her. Then he guided her toward it. Even then she could not seem to see it. Even though it was lying there fully exposed. Finally, he pointed it out to her. "What's that over there?" he asked. "Probably just an oyster shell, but you might as well check it out."

She leaned over and picked it up. "No," she said without much excitement, "it is an arrowhead. But not a very good one." Then she turned and slung it out into the Bay. It skipped once and sank.

"What are you doing!?" Roy asked.

She turned and looked him squarely in the eye. "I'm teaching you a lesson, young man, one that will be very valuable to you in later life: Never treat a woman like a child, even if she's acting childish. *Especially* if she's acting childish."

"Okay," Roy said. What else could he say? He didn't know how to talk to women.

"Of course, if it had been the pretty one," Evelyn said, "I would have kept it. That's the second lesson: every woman has her price."

Roy nodded. He felt like he was back in grade school. Who was he kidding anyway? Evelyn was out of his league. She was a woman of the world, and he'd only been out of Virginia a couple of times. "Well," he finally said, looking at his watch, "I guess I'd better be getting back. That tide isn't going to get much higher. In fact, it'll be falling soon."

"Would you like something to drink before you go? I've got a Coke in my bag. Don't know how cold it is."

"Sure," Roy said. "Why not?" It was hot, and he'd been out there a long time.

They walked back up to where she'd left her bag. He helped her spread her beach towel on the sand. When she opened the Coke, which had been in the sun, foam spurted from the top of the bottle. Evelyn held the bottle to her mouth until the foam settled. When she handed the bottle to Roy, she was laughing and her eyes were watering from the carbonation. Soda was running down her chest. "What a mess," she said.

The Coke was warm, but it still tasted good to Roy. Better than good, because the flavor of the soda was mixed with the taste of Evelyn's lipstick. In fact, it was the best Coke Roy had ever tasted; he knew he would remember it for a long time. When he handed it back to her, she smiled.

"You look like you just got kissed," she said.

"What?"

"You've got lipstick all over your mouth." She wiped his lips with her thumb.

Even her thumb tasted good. "Well," Roy said, collecting himself. "It was nice seeing you again."

"Before you go, will you do me a favor?" Evelyn asked.

"What's that?"

She tossed him the tube of suntan lotion and lay face down on the towel. "Do my back," she said. "Please."

Roy looked at his watch and then down at Evelyn's back. How long could it take to do a back? "Sure," he said, kneeling down beside her on the towel. He squeezed some of the white lotion into the palm of his hand and sniffed it. Somehow it didn't smell the same in his hand as it did on her. It was nice, but it wasn't the same.

"Before you start," Evelyn said, "make sure you've got all the sand off your hands. That's very important."

"Okay," he said, wiping his hands on his bathing suit.

He started at the pale top part of her neck near the hairline and worked his way down to the base of her neck and out onto her shoulders. Her skin was surprisingly smooth and soft. He thought because it was already tan it might be leathery and tough, but it was not at all. He re-lathered his hands and covered her shoulder blades and upper spine. She wriggled her upper back the way his cat sometimes did when he rubbed her. "You didn't tell me you were an expert," Evelyn said.

"I'm not," Roy said.

"Such sensitive hands."

He got more lotion and moved down to the middle and lower portions of her back.

"Wait," she said.

Roy flinched. He thought maybe he had gone too far or she had read his mind, but that wasn't it. She reached back with both hands, deftly undid the top of her bathing suit and pulled the loose ends down out of the way.

"Mustn't have any lines," Evelyn said. "I like a nice even tan."

"Right," Roy said.

Now her whole back was exposed. Except for the skimpy bottom to her bathing suit, it was as if she were naked. "Forget about that," Roy told himself. "Concentrate on the job." He tried to approach her lower back the same as if he had been caulking and coppering the bottom of a skiff. You had to make sure every inch was covered, every nook and cranny, the furrows between her ribs, the low places between the ridges of her spine, all of it.

He caught a glimpse of his watch, glanced over at the tide and remembered his promise to Lester. But the tide was already falling. If he left now, he'd probably still be too late to pull the skiff up. Then neither job would get done right. And wasn't Evelyn a relative too? Wasn't she entitled to the same courtesy and consideration as Lester? Of course she was.

"Want me to do the legs?" Roy blurted, sounding, he hoped, like a young professional, a handyman or maybe a house painter.

"Ahm, sure," Evelyn said, "if you'd like."

The supply of lotion was dangerously low. He rolled the tube from the bottom the way you would a tube of toothpaste. If he had to, he'd borrow lotion from her back. He'd used enough there. Her back glistened like polished copper.

He started with the soles of her feet—burned soles could be very painful—and worked quickly up to her ankles and then her calves. Her calves were strong and muscular, like a boy's only nicer, smoother and no hair except a fine stubble that reminded him of how the marsh grass felt to the bottoms of his feet. He shut his eyes and imagined he was wandering back among the tidal pools looking for arrowheads. Soon he found himself at the soft places behind her knees, and then he was above her knees in new and unfamiliar territory, where the hair was no longer shaved. It was the farthest he'd ever been with a woman, and even if he'd gotten there under false pretenses, and even if she was his cousin, it still counted.

His fingers moved tentatively along until he felt Evelyn take his wrists affectionately but firmly in her grasp. He felt disappointed and relieved at the same time. He withdrew his hands and helped her fix the top of her bathing suit because she was having trouble doing it alone. Without looking at him, Evelyn sat up and groped around in her beach bag until she found her cigarettes. Her hands were shaking. "You don't smoke yet, do you?" Her voice was shaky too.

"No," Roy said. "Thanks anyway."

She sat with her arms wrapped around her knees; she still wouldn't look at him. "What about that skiff?" she said. "I thought you had some work to do." Then Roy realized she was crying.

"Look," Roy said, "I'm sorry if I upset you."

She turned toward him. Her eyes were red and filled with tears, but she was smiling. "No, no, no," she said. "Don't apologize. You did fine. You were sweet and kind and a little horny, sure, but so what? You're supposed to be at your age, and I encouraged it, but that's not the point. It's the other that threw me."

"I don't get it."

"I'm sure you don't." She inhaled and sighed. "See—and don't take this personally—but I operate under the principle that all men are bastards. They're born that way; they'll always be that way, and I let it go at that. It's neat, clean and it's not all that inaccurate. And then to be reminded that men too—men!—start off in such a state of innocence! It just hurts, that's all. It's easier the other way. Safer." She inhaled and then flicked her cigarette toward the water.

"Innocence?" Roy said. He certainly didn't feel innocent. He'd lied to his uncle and practically raped his cousin.

"Relatively speaking. Relative to what comes later."

"And where'd you get the idea that all men are bastards anyway?" Roy said.

"Where do you think?"

"I don't know."

"Oh, Roy," she said, "you are sweet." She leaned over, rested her head on his shoulder and draped an arm across his knees. "I just wish the rest of the world could be like this farm, this beach. Don't you?"

"That would be nice," Roy said, but he didn't realize then that the farm was so different from the rest of the world. He would always remember that this was where he heard it first and that it was Evelyn who told him. And even though she made it sound like common knowledge, it felt like she'd confided in him. He put his arm around her shoulders and rested his head against hers. They sat like that for a long time, neither of them talking.

When it finally really was time for Roy to leave, he stood up, reached into his pocket and removed the arrowhead, the one he knew she wanted. She folded his fingers around it and squeezed his fist. "But I want you to have it," he said. "I do."

"I know you do, and I accept it. In fact, I insist on having it. But I want it to remain in your collection for safekeeping. A stone of such 'archaeological interest' shouldn't be separated from the others. You can label it, 'On loan from Evelyn Harmon Hoyt.'"

"Okay," Roy said. What else could he say? It was the perfect solution. "You're pretty smart, aren't you?"

She laughed. "Oh, brother."

The way she said goodbye, with a warm hug, a kiss on the cheek and then a quick friendly one on the lips, was more like she was saying goodbye, not to her little cousin, but to one of her men. Roy liked that very much, and when he got home, he labeled the arrowhead exactly according to her request.

POLLUTION NOSTALGIA

Fifty-five years ago, a trip to the dump for Uncle Ben meant loading the garbage into the skiff and motoring out to the Middle Ground of Dividing Creek. Even then, Ben was meticulous in his disposal of waste: glass bottles were carefully broken with a hammer so they would sink to the bottom. Eventually, the pieces would wash up on the beach, their surfaces pocked and smoky, the edges rounded, magically transformed by the Bay's alchemy from garbage into "sea glass," nature's jewelry.

The tin cans had a less exotic life cycle: they corroded and rusted into their basic elements, but Ben made sure that they sank. Table scraps, grapefruit rinds, chicken bones and any other leftovers were feasts for crabs. Papers were burned onshore, and plastic, in those days, was virtually nonexistent.

Far out in the Bay, a similar process occurred on a larger scale: tankers and freighters heading to Baltimore dumped their garbage directly into the Bay. We could not actually see them do it; so far away were they that on calm days only their superstructures protruded above the horizon, and on rough days nothing at all. But walking the beach we would find their flotsam and jetsam—wooden crates with foreign script, bottles, lumber, boat cushions and, particularly treasured, intact light bulbs. Arrowheads were our number one quarry when we walked the beach, but when we carried our air rifles, which was often, light bulbs were a close second.

A light bulb bobbing in the waves made a challenging target, and there was never an argument about whether a light bulb was hit or not, as there might have been with a heavier glass bottle, which could absorb surprising amounts of shot. Old soda bottles were notoriously hard to break, but airtight light bulbs, the only kind that made it ashore, never sank on their own, and when hit by a BB, they did not simply break; they exploded with a very satisfying and definitive "pop." We never worried about later cutting our feet on the broken pieces, because we understood what sand and waves would do to glass. The idea that the BBs themselves might have been considered a form of pollution, as lead shot later was, would have seemed ludicrous. BBs and lead shot were miniscule, and the Bay was vast—a convenient repository of waste and an inexhaustible source of fish, crabs, oysters and waterfowl.

Appalling though it may appear in retrospect, these were truly pollution's "good old days." In fact, it is hardly fair to call what was done then "pollution"; it was more like a form of littering and might even be considered a primitive version of recycling: rust returning mineral iron and tin to the water, table scraps turned into seafood and bottles transformed into lovely colored glass. In those innocent days, air pollution was the odor of the fish factory in Reedville or, with a different wind, the smell of the paper mill in West Point. Acid rain, mercury, thermal pollution, global warming—these phrases had not yet entered our lexicon. Lucky us.

I would date the loss of innocence to 1975 and the discovery of Kepone in the James River—three years after the Clean Water Act. Kepone was a pesticide manufactured in Hopewell, Virginia, on the banks of the James River. The residue of the manufacturing process was dumped down the storm drains or poured into the air. Eventually, the plant workers developed inexplicable tremors, which an observant doctor traced back to Allied Chemical, the makers of Kepone. The Environmental Protection Agency investigated and found Kepone in the air, water, in the workers' tissues, in fish and oysters and in the James River sediment. Testing showed that Kepone was neurotoxic, carcinogenic and persistent, meaning that it was very difficult to remove from the environment.

Not everyone was convinced of Kepone's deleterious effects. My cousin Hal, no longer able to sell bluefish because of Kepone in their tissues, was forced to bail them overboard alive. He hated doing it. "They look awright to me," he said, and they did look all right. They looked as frisky and snappy as ever, ready to cut a finger or a fishing line, but by then I'd had enough education to know that this time Hal was probably wrong. Hal knew just about all there was to know about fish and crabs and oysters and the Bay, but I was afraid that pollution technology had

A drainage ditch on Bluff Point, 2004. *Ida Hall photo.*

Same drainage ditch seen from the Bay, 2004. *Ida Hall photo.*

Same ditch pouring muddy water into the Chesapeake, 2004. This is not non-point source pollution. *Ida Hall photo.*

passed him by. Pollution had gotten subtle, insidious (and would soon get more so). Just because a fish looked, smelled and tasted fine, and just because ingesting it did not make you sick immediately, that did not mean it was safe to eat.

The Kepone story had the makings of a Hollywood movie. There was a villain, Allied Chemical, and a hero—the doctor who traced the neurological symptoms to their source—and a sort of happy ending: they stopped making Kepone and an effective treatment, cholestyramine, was found for the workers' illness. Fade out and roll the credits. If only it could be said that the fish, crabs and oysters of the Chesapeake had lived happily ever after, but sadly, that was not the case.

In fact, since the mid-1970s, there has been a steady decline in the health of the Bay. Pollution is worse; finfish populations have plummeted; wild oysters have practically disappeared; and this time the enemy is far more diffuse, elusive and dangerous than Kepone. "Non-point source pollution" only sounds innocuous, and now there is no one to blame except everyone. If you drive a car, if you pave your drive, if you fertilize your lawn, if you even have a lawn, if you farm and fertilize your crops, if you raise animals, if you shop in malls—you contribute to non-point source pollution. It is herbicides and pesticides, of course, but also phosphorous and nitrogen, which cause algae blooms that deplete the Bay of oxygen, leaving "dead zones" where nothing lives.

According to *U.S. Water News* online, in July 2005, a third of the Chesapeake was a "dead zone." Every issue of the *Bay Journal* seems more alarming than the last. The grass beds are either not returning or are returning exceedingly slowly; oyster restoration, if possible, is vastly more complicated than simply introducing resistant species; blue crabs are hanging on but barely. It is hard not to be discouraged. The problems are enormous, and as of 2009 the numbers—pollutants and fish populations—have not turned around. On the other hand...

Implicit in the discouraging data is at least some good news: the number of people and organizations dedicated to improving the health of the Chesapeake has skyrocketed. The same giant population accused of "loving the Bay to death" has risen up in the Bay's defense. If many people making small contributions to pollution cause the problem, is it not at least theoretically possible that small changes by that same huge population could undo at least a portion of the damage? And if huge numbers of people mean massive pollution, they also mean considerable political clout, which unfortunately is also required.

The most prominent of the nonprofit organizations supporting restoration of the Bay include the Chesapeake Bay Foundation (Save the Bay) and the Alliance for the Chesapeake Bay, publishers of the *Bay Journal*, a free monthly newsletter, a must-read for anyone with an interest in the region. It is highly entertaining, contains tons of information and is free of guilt trips or political diatribes. The alliance does not litigate; it focuses on "collaboration and consensus-building."

The Chesapeake Bay Foundation, however, does litigate. In fact, in January 2009, it sued the Environmental Protection Agency, not in pursuit of new rules and regulations, but simply demanding that it enforce the Clean Water Act (on the books since 1972) and the Chesapeake 2000 agreement. Imagine that.

The Chesapeake Bay Program is an agency most of us already support (with tax dollars). Its "free" online news service provides links to daily headlines of Chesapeake-related articles.

There are many other organizations working on behalf of the Chesapeake with contact information readily available online. In fact, if you charted the rate of the proliferation of these groups in the last few decades, you would find something like the mirror image of those other, sadder graphics of rising pollution and falling fish populations, and in that image and in that mirror, you might even find a measure of hope.

BILLY HAYNIE:
A HOPEFUL FUTURE

In July 2008, William H. Haynie of Reedville applied to the Virginia Marine Resources Commission for permission to locate two pound nets, eight hundred feet long, in the vicinity of Fleeton Point not far from the Great Wicomico River. As there was no opposition, permission was granted without a hearing.

A few months later, Mr. Haynie requested permission to locate a third pound net, this one four hundred feet long, in the vicinity of Hughlett's Point, just north of Dividing Creek. Hughlett Point was the site of a two-hundred-acre Natural Area Preserve. Fourteen letters were submitted in opposition to his proposal and only six in support. Of interest, not a single letter came from the Department of Conservation and Recreation, which maintains the Natural Preserve. Of even more interest to me, and more troubling, was that four of the opposing letters were from members of my own family, descendants of commercial fishermen, of pound netters. The gist of the opposing letters was that the net would be an "eyesore," a "hazard to navigation." A "pristine" view would be spoiled; the net would attract birds and "all their mess." Dead fish would wash onto the shore of the preserve. A net might cause "erosion" and generally be a "public nuisance."

Times change, of course, but how on earth had it come to this? How had the Chesapeake reached the point at which a pound net was an "eyesore" but a lush, manicured lawn leading from an expensive home to an elaborate dock and boat lift was evidently a thing of beauty? How had the once iconic Chesapeake Bay watermen, the subject of coffee table books and calendar art, been reduced to pillagers and plunderers of the Bay, no better than pirates? And finally, who was this William H. Haynie, and what in the world made him think that there was a fishery worth harvesting, much less fighting over? Did he not know that the Bay was on its deathbed? Had he not heard that oysters were disease-ridden and dying? That crabs and finfish were all moribund or worse? That the grass beds were depleted and the oxygen levels were low? If he had heard, he did not seem to believe.

"It's all coming back," he said on the damp, cool April morning in 2009 when I visited.

I had asked about the heavy strike of oysters on his pilings; some were dead, of course, but remarkably, many were alive. Where had so much natural strike come from? I wondered to myself. Perhaps it came from the same mysterious place as Billy's optimism, from some poorly understood life force of the Bay. While politicians and biologists fussed and fumed, somewhere in the Bay oysters were asserting their own resilience, staging their own rebellion and—to hell with the experts and pessimists—were reproducing, releasing spat into the polluted, disease-ridden waters of the Chesapeake. A few even survived. For all our knowledge of the Bay, there is much we do not know; and in our ignorance there is room for hope and room, thank goodness, for people like Billy Haynie. (It turns out that the source of those oysters might be less mysterious, but even more exciting than I thought: an August 2009 article in *Science* reported on an oyster restoration project of "unprecedented" scope with very promising results in the Great Wicomico River, at the mouth of which Fleeton happens to sit.)

Billy is a tall, lean, dark-haired man of thirty-four, but already his back has undergone two operations. "My back is good now," he said. As I said, he is an optimist. A Chesapeake Bay waterman in the twenty-first century would have to be.

Billy started crabbing at the age of eight; his brother once worked on the water and his father too, but in his family that's as far back as the fishing went. However, Reedville has been a commercial fishing town since the late nineteenth century, when Elijah Reed moved down from Maine. There is now a splendid Waterman's Museum, dedicated to the preservation of photographs, fishing boats, models and other artifacts of the commercial fishing industry. Omega Protein, Reedville's last standing menhaden factory, bills itself as North America's largest producer of Omega-3 fish oil and, therefore, a "heart healthy" company. It owns the fleet of purse seiners that, guided by their "spotter" planes, plies the Bay and Atlantic Ocean in pursuit of menhaden, which are "rendered" into fish oil, cat food and fertilizer. In

Left: Billy Haynie heading out from Fleeton, 2009.

Below: Billy's pound net off Fleeton Point, an "eyesore" to some, but not to everyone.

earlier times, menhaden oil competed with whale oil and made men rich. So it is not surprising that someone who grew up in the area might think of fishing for menhaden as a livelihood, and, in fact, menhaden were Billy Haynie's target species. His, however, were not "rendered," but were frozen and later sold as crab bait.

As we left the dock and headed out of the creek and into the Bay, I could feel a familiar anticipation build. It had been thirty-five years since I had seen a pound net fished, but the excitement was only slightly less, and that was not so much due to age as to the water temperature: cold water would limit the fish species we were likely to see. The crabs were not moving yet, and the spot, croaker and trout had not yet arrived. Menhaden, with perhaps a few herring, would be the most that we would hope for.

Like most good fishermen, Billy Haynie is an innovator. In the simplest terms, a pound net consists of a several-hundred-foot-long leader connected to a heart-shaped "false pound" that guides the fish through a funnel into the "pound" itself (also called a "pocket") from which the fish are bailed—dip netted—into the boat. Traditionally, the leader is held in place by dozens of stakes, all of which must be cut from small pines, limbed, sharpened and then pumped or driven into the bottom. It is heavy, difficult work, the work that is rarely captured in calendar art, but Billy replaced most of his leader stakes with seine net corks and secured his bottom line with a series of anchors, thereby reducing the number of stakes required. His proposed Hughlett Point net would have no leader at all, but two four-hundred-foot "wings" flaring away from the pound at angles, like a huge false pound. This had never been done before.

Most older pound netters, such as Hal, towed a small skiff behind a large work boat. The skiff would fit inside the pocket, and from it the men would bail the fish into the hold of the large boat. Billy fishes from a twenty-one-foot Carolina Skiff, which is small enough to fit (barely) inside his pound but large enough, most days, to hold his catch. He has, therefore, eliminated the need for a large work boat and large boat payments.

When we arrived at the pocket, no fish were visible, because fish hold deep until the net is raised. Billy slackened the top lines, slid the skiff into the pocket and began to work slack into the net. Hal always had two helpers to help raise the heavy pocket and its load of fish, but Billy Haynie fishes alone. As he raised the heavy net, he secured the slack with bungee cords, which functioned as an extra set of hands. The first indication of fish came as a subtle darkening of the water. "We got a little color," Billy said. Then the

Hal and his men, 1960s. *Photo by Grayson Mattingly, Ditchley, Virginia.*

dark water came alive as a conglomeration of swirling shapes and flashes of silver. He secured the net and began bailing.

It was only when the first netfuls of fish landed, flopping and skittering, into the boat that what appeared to be a homogeneous school of menhaden separated into individual fish of several species: a few herring, grey perch and small flounder—all very much alive. The flounder were too small to sell and had to be released at once, not an easy task, since they are flat, slippery and stick to the wet planks like suction cups. The rounded edge of dip net would not slide under them; they had to be pried up individually and lifted out by hand. But small fish are the future, and these were handled with care.

Soon there were a few hundred pounds of menhaden flopping about, and Billy was done. He released the slack net, backed the skiff out of the pocket, secured the funnel and other lines and off we went. He would fish the second net tomorrow.

At the dock, the fish were shoveled onto a conveyor belt, dumped into cartons and stashed in the walk-in dockside freezer to await the beginning of crab season. There is little, if any, romance in this part of the operation. The fish have been identified and were dead; the suspense was gone—except the final mystery, the bottom line: how much were they worth? Maybe $100, Billy supposed, maybe not. Meanwhile, there were the expenses of gas, boat, net, dock lease, electricity, etc., etc.

Billy Haynie fishes his pound net alone.

Billy Haynie bailing fish from his Fleeton Point net, 2009.

I should not have been surprised that our conversation at the dock turned to finance, specifically the stock market. Billy traded stocks online, and his retirement fund, like many in the spring of 2009, had taken a hit. Sometimes, when we romanticize (or demonize) the lives of the Chesapeake Bay watermen, we lose sight of the fact that they are simply trying to make a living. Surely commercial fishing is not just a job—it's more than that—but it is a job, and Billy has a wife and two young daughters, and he was determined to make his living on the water, regardless of how pleasure boaters and sport fishermen might have felt about it.

As he began transferring the fish from the conveyor belt into cardboard cartons, a big sedan pulled up and a gray-haired lady stepped out. "Uh-oh," said Billy. "You are in for a rare treat now."

The lady walked gingerly across the gravel drive, small plastic bag in hand. Billy makes the introductions. Her name was Alice. She stepped back and sized me up. "You're not one of those environmentalists, are you?" She made "environmentalist" sound like a bad word.

Though I don't think of myself that way, her feistiness led me to say, "Well, I guess in some ways I am. I would like to see a cleaner Bay, wouldn't you?" Who could argue against a cleaner Bay?

After Billy assured her that I was on his side, the side of commercial fishermen, she backed off, and they tended to the business at hand: herring roe. "I just want one," she said, but he gave her three.

He bent a dead herring backward until its belly broke open to reveal two bright-orange skeins of roe, which he dumped directly into her bag. Then two more and she was on her way. "Thank you," she said with a little wave.

Cleanup time. "That's the trouble," Billy said. "You work two hours in the morning and you go around smelling like fish for the rest of the day."

"So?" He said nothing, but I got the feeling that smelling like fish was not quite as socially acceptable as it once had been.

The Virginia Marine Resources Commission (VMRC), which meets monthly in Newport News, consists of nine white men all with some connection to saltwater fishing. There is one commercial fisherman from the Eastern Shore, a professor of ecology, several recreational fishermen (one of whom is designated as the "official" recreational fishing representative) and several businessmen with connections to boating and aquaculture.

The agenda was long, and Billy Haynie's proposal came after lunch, when people were lethargic, and the opposition never really materialized. The VMRC staff member summarized the opposition's written comments—

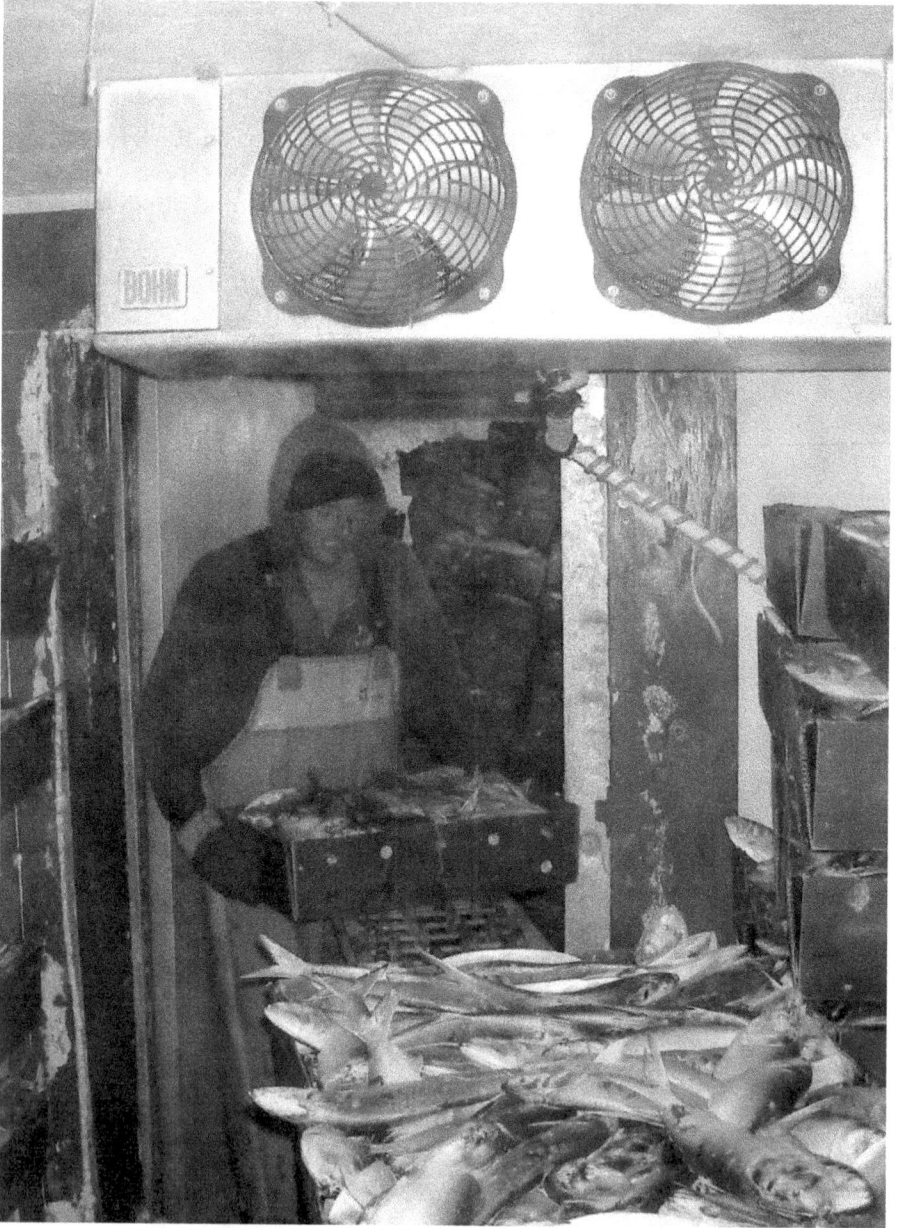

Billy Haynie in his dockside freezer putting away the day's catch for crab season.

Ida Hall testifying before the Virginia Marine Resources Commission in support of Billy Haynie's proposed pound net, 2009.

eyesore, navigational hazard, dead fish, live but messy birds, detriment to water quality and proximity to the Natural Area Preserve—but noted that he had twice solicited input from the Department of Conservation and Recreation, which maintains the preserve, and had not received one comment. "I can only take that to mean that they don't have an issue with the trap." Also, one individual who lived in the area and volunteered at the preserve wrote in support of Mr. Haynie, whom she knew to be a "good fisherman" who would take care of his nets. In the end, the VMRC staff was "inclined to support" Mr. Haynie's application.

The one opponent who did speak, a recreational fisherman and charter boat captain, did so in order to retract his opposition and to apologize to Mr. Haynie. Since the trap would not be located on his favorite fishing grounds, as he had first believed, he had no objection.

Ken Smith, president of the Virginia Waterman's Association, is well known to the VMRC, and in his support of Mr. Haynie he compared a pound net to the 1,800-foot pier across a "pristine" marsh that was recently approved. Then he asked, rhetorically, which was the real "eyesore"?

My sister Ida, speaking in support of the proposal, recounted the fond memories of the summer of 1964 when each morning she went out with her cousin Hal to fish his traps. "It changed my life," she said, and over the years observing pound netters taught her respect for the resource and respect for other fishermen, both commercial and sport fishermen.

The commission approved Billy's application unanimously and with very little debate.

Afterward, Billy seemed relieved and grateful for the support he received. I relayed Steve Proctor's offer to show him the Deep Hole trap site, fished for so many years by Steve's grandfather and after him by Steve's Uncle Hal. Billy would be welcome to place a trap there; we would love to see it. Steve has the same fond memories that Ida has, that I have. To us, a pound net is not only not an eyesore; it's like a natural object, an indicator of life, a vital sign. A healthy Bay sprouts stakes like saplings—stakes marking pound nets, peeler traps, oyster shore and duck blinds—and in such waters brightly colored crab pot buoys bloom like wildflowers. If some of us romanticize the lives of watermen—and we do—it is in part because we are reminded of our childhoods, but it is that memory of a healthy Bay that really makes us sigh.

SOURCES

QUAIL

Fies, Mike. "Virginia's Bobwhite Legacy: A History of the Bobwhite Quail and Its Management." *Virginia Wildlife Magazine*, March 1997. www.dgif.virginia.gov/quail/quaillegacy.asp.

Virginia Department of Game and Inland Fisheries. "Northern Bobwhite Quail Action Plan for Virginia." http://www.dgif.virginia.gov/wildlife/quail/action-plan/quail-action-plan.pdf.

WATERFOWLING

Illinois State Museum. "Punt Gunning." http://www.museum.state.il.us/River/Web/Harvesting/waterfowltools.

"Odd Survival of the Punt Gun." http://sportsillustrated.cnn.com/vault/article/magazine/MAG1076735/index.htm.

Punt Gunning in England. http://www.wildfowling.com/Puntgunning/puntgunning.htm.

OYSTERS

Chesapeake Bay Program. chesapeakebay.net/status_oysterharvest.

Mariners' Museum, Newport News, VA. "Oysters." http://www.mariners-museum.org/chesapeakebay/waterman/wat009.html.

Sources

Northeaster Regional Aquaculture Center Fact sheet No. 200–1993. University of Massachusetts, Dartmouth.

Schulte, D.M., R.P. Burke and R.N. Lipicius. "Unprecedented Restoration of a Native Oyster Metapopulation." *Science* 325 (2009), 1124.

Pollution

Chesapeake Bay Journal. "After 20 Years, Kepone Still a Part of River Life…" (September 1995). bayjournal.com/article.cfm?article=999.

Environmental Protection Agency. "Non-Point Source." www.epa.gov/owow/nps/qa.html.

Virginia Commonwealth University. "Kepone." vcu.edu/engweb/Rivertime/chp17.htm.

Menhaden/Reedville

Omega Protein Corporation. omegaproteininc.com.

Reedville Fishermen's Museum. rfmuseum.com.

Virginia Institute of Marine Science. "Menhaden Background." vims.edu/menhaden/background.html.

Wikipedia. "Reedville, Virginia." en.wikipedia.org/wiki/Reedville,_Virginia.

Other

Alliance for the Chesapeake Bay
530 East Main Street, Suite 200
Richmond, VA 23218
804-775-0951
acbva@acb-online.org
http://www.acb-online.org

Chesapeake Bay Foundation
Capitol Place
1108 East Main Street, Suite 1600
Richmond, VA 23219
804-648-4011
cbf.org

Chesapeake Bay Program
40 Severn Avenue, Suite 109
Annapolis, MD 21403
1-800-YOUR-BAY
chesapeakebay.net